A HISTORY OF POLITICAL INSTITUTIONS IN JAPAN

A HISTORY OF
POLITICAL INSTITUTIONS
IN JAPAN

RYŌSUKE ISHII

UNIVERSITY OF TOKYO PRESS

This book was originally published by the University of Tokyo Press in 1972 under the title *Nihon kokkashi*.

English translation © 1980 by
THE JAPAN FOUNDATION

UTP   3021–27133–5149
ISBN   0–86008–261–X

Printed in Japan

CONTENTS

PREFACE

This volume is an outline of the history of political institutions in Japan. It was originally intended to cover all aspects of Japan's legal history. But, as limitations of space have made that impossible, only matters of public law are dealt with here. For the same reason, its coverage does not go beyond the restoration of national independence following World War II.

In the study of legal history, it is, of course, very important to disclose the structure of the law of each period, but the fundamental structure of legal history itself involves more than this. Just as legal systems must have structure if legal history is to be considered a scholarly field, so history itself must also have structure. The flow of social events after prehistory is therefore divided up in accordance with a definite standard into a number of periods. This periodization does not come about of its own accord: it is constructed by historians. Accordingly, periodizations differ, depending on the historian. The length of a historical period is reckoned in the same way as time in the natural sciences, but periodization itself is a historical concept, not derived from the natural sciences. To admit this is to assert, all the more strongly, that it is the structure of history, in the most fundamental sense.

Readers of this volume will note that the periodization scheme employed here differs markedly from those usually found in Japanese histories. This periodization is based on the author's conviction that the course of historical development proceeds in a wavelike motion. The flow of historical time is taken to be a series of fluctuations, and one such "wave" is understood to constitute a single period. In this periodization, therefore, each period has a distinctive feature and can be subdivided into a beginning phase, when the special feature is developing, a middle phase, when it is at its fullest florescence, and an ending phase, when it declines. Applying these standards to the state, we arrive at the following:

Early Period	Archaic	The Tribal (Religious) State
	Ancient	The *Ritsuryō* State
Medieval Period		The Early Feudal State
Early Modern Period		The Centralized Feudal State (The Purely Feudal State)
Modern Period		The Modern Monarchic State
Contemporary Period		The Modern Democratic State (The Democratic State)

In the archaic period, as identified here, the distinctive feature was the undifferentiated union of law and religion. In the ancient period, it was the *ritsuryō* legal system, actually a centralized, bureaucratic political order received from China. In the medieval period, it was the system of estate feudalism or *shōen* feudalism, and in the early modern period, it was statist feudalism or *bakufu* feudalism. The modern period was characterized by monarchical constitutionalism, and the present is characterized by constitutional democracy.

Since the archaic period was one when law and (indigenous) religon were unseparated, and the ancient period was a time when they clearly were separated, combining them both into a single early period seems at first glance to be without meaning. Since, however, the archaic period is, as it were, the mother, and the ancient period, the father, that produced the medieval period, the it would seem logical that, as both stand in a parental relationship to the medieval period, they should be combined into a single unit, the early period, preceding it.

The undifferentiated union of law and religion that characterized the archaic period is contrasted with later times when religion and law were separate; so as to draw a corresponding contrast between the political designations of the ancient and later periods, the archaic political community could be best called a religious system of political power. The medieval period, coming between the early and feudal societies, and the modern period, with its strongly feudal coloration, coming between the feudal and contemporary societies, constitute transitional periods, showing most clearly the process of development. To a greater or lesser degree, some connection to the feudal system persisted from the medieval period through the modern. Liberation from feudalism came only at the onset of the contemporary period.* This means that the contemporary period has begun an entirely new era in the history of Japan.

Because of Japan's special geographic condition, separated from the Asian continent by the Korean peninsula, the influence of foreign law has been slight; nor have there been any natural political dangers grave enough to impede natural development. The result was autonomous development with rich achievements. In the ancient period, Chinese law exerted a strong influence. But it was accepted exactly at the point where the native law was in a state of decline and, after its period of florescence, itself declined. It did not, therefore, in any way impede the typical wavelike pattern of development. The other example of the influence of alien law is that of European and American law during the modern period. In this case too, however, the foreign law was received at a time when the native law of the early modern period had declined, and the wavelike pattern of development was not disturbed.

The dividing of historical periods into early, middle, and late sections is something I have devised in the context of legal history. In my view, however, law is that which regulates social activities and organization, so that legal history makes up the skeletal framework of history itself. Of course, just as a body cannot operate on the basis of its skeleton alone, history moves only as a totality, and legal history cannot claim any peculiar importance. However, just as the human body can be divided up by reference to the parts of the skeleton, legal development can be used as a standard

* The reader wishing to pursue this concept of feudalism in more detail should see the author's article "Japanese Feudalism" ("Nihon Hoken Seido") in the November 1978 issue of *Acta Asiatica* (published by Toyo Gakkai [Institute of Eastern Culture], no. 35, pp. 1–29).

by which to assess historical development. I have already applied a periodization based on legal history in my *Nihonshi Gairon (An Outline of Japanese History*, 1953).

In any case, as stated above, Japanese legal history and its development can be explained clearly in terms of the wave theory of history; in this sense, Japanese legal history (and, more broadly, Japanese history itself) assuredly shows one form—and an important form—of historical development in the general history of mankind.

This book was first written and published for a Japanese audience, nearly a decade ago. Translating it into English and making it accessible to an audience unfamiliar with the nuances of Japanese history seemed a formidable task indeed when it was begun. Without the help and efforts of three scholars who worked on the translation, it would be a task still uncompleted. The author is very grateful for the contributions of Kuwabara Makoto of the National Diet Library, Gordon Berger of the University of Southern California, and Cornelius J. Kiley of Villanova University.

Mount Miwa, located in the southeastern part of the Nara Basin, Nara Prefecture (see the map on page 15). This area is thought to have been the site of the ancient Yamatai state, and later of Emperor Sujin's palace.

(courtesy of Ōkami Shrine)

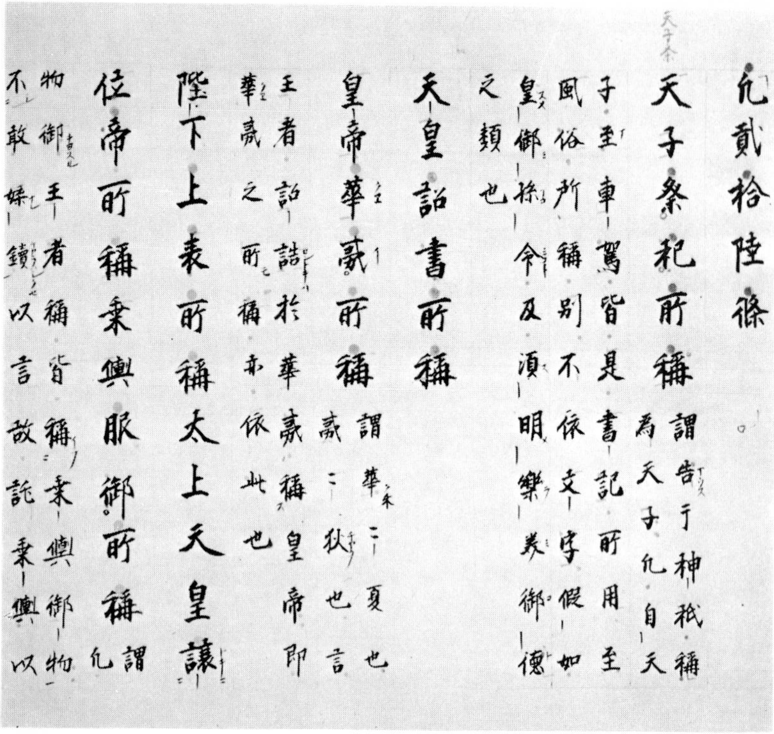

儿貳拾陸條

天子条祀所稱　謂告于神祇稱
　為天子凡自至天
子至車駕皆是書記所用至
風俗所稱別不依文字假如
皇御孫命及須明樂羹御德
之類也

天皇詔書所稱

皇帝華羲所稱　謂華二夏也
　謂二狄也言
王者詔詰於華嘉稱皇帝即
華羲之所稱亦依此也

陛下上表所稱太上天皇讓

位帝所稱秉輿服御所稱謂
物御王者稱皆秉輿御物
不敢媒鑪以言故詫秉輿以

A portion of the *Ryō no gige,* a commentary on Chinese law published during
the Heian era. The part shown here indicates that the ruler who was called
tennō in imperial pronouncements was generally referred to by the Chinese
title *kōtei.*
(Momijiyama manuscript, courtesy of Kokuritsu Kobunshokan)

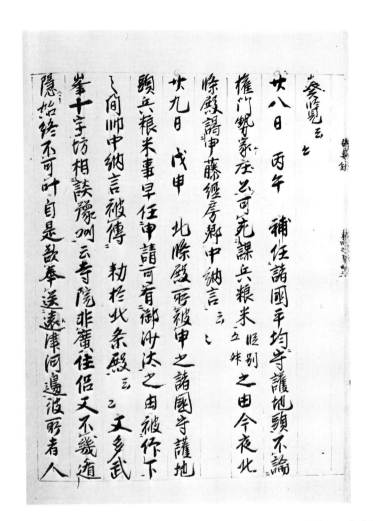

A portion of the *Azuma-kagami*, a history of Japan written around the end of the thirteenth century. The passage shown here describes how Hōjō Tokimasa, on behalf of Minamoto Yoritomo, petitioned the emperor to recognize the *bakufu* appointments of local officials (*shugo* and *jitō*). The next day, according to this account, the court ordered that the appointments be recognized, and an imperial order to that effect was issued the following week.

(Hōjō manuscript, courtesy of Kokuritsu Kobunshokan)

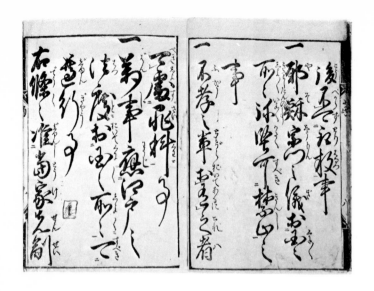

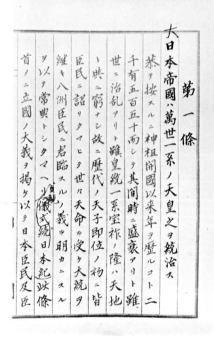

A portion of the 1663 *Buke sho-hatto*, the Tokugawa *bakufu*'s regulations applying to the *daimyō*. The article which begins on the left-hand page states that all *daimyō* are to regard the *bakufu*'s legislative pronouncements as the law of the land.

(Ita manuscript, courtesy of Okuno Hikoroku)

Draft of the Meiji Constitution submitted to the Privy Council in 1888. The drafters had called the nation "Nippon Teikoku" (the Japanese Empire), but since the draft of the Imperial Household Law called it "Dai Nippon Teikoku" (the Great Japanese Empire), the draft manuscript was corrected by the Privy Council to read "Dai Nippon Teikoku," as can be seen in the first line of the text.

(Hishoruisan kankokai duplicate manuscript)

A HISTORY OF POLITICAL INSTITUTIONS IN JAPAN

THE UNIFICATION OF THE *UJI* AND THE FORMATION OF THE *AMENOSHITA-SHIROSHIMESU-SUMERAMIKOTO*

Jōdai, or Archaic Period, *ca.* 250 B.C. to 603 A.D.

It is difficult to discuss the prehistory of Japan with any degree of certainty. Indeed, the prevailing theory before World War II was that there was no Paleolithic age in Japan. In the postwar period, however, relics from Paleolithic times have been found in many places, proving beyond doubt that there was such an age. We know something more of the Neolithic age, which was represented in Japan by earthenware of the Jōmon type and is hence called the Jōmon period.* The Neolithic inhabitants of Japan did not yet practice agriculture. That much we know; we have, however, virtually no knowledge of the political institutions characterizing these two ages. Thus, any history of Japanese political institutions must begin with the Yayoi** culture that followed them.

Japanese law in the archaic period was characterized by its very close relationship with religion. The first part of this period, from the second or third century B.C. to about the end of the second century A.D., coincided with the era in which Yayoi culture flourished. We must presume that primitive religion governed every aspect of society during this era. In the middle part of the archaic period, during the third and fourth centuries, religious authority

---

* The Jōmon period is so called because of the rope imprints (*jōmon*) that often appear on the pottery of this period. The markings were produced by pressing ropes of twisted fiber into the clay. The pottery has a blackened appearance and comes in a rich variety of forms.

** The name Yayoi derives from the name of the place where remains of the culture were first discovered. The vessels dating from this period are a dull reddish or greenish brown and lack much variety of form.

constituted the basis of the political power employed by the emperors in unifying various independent kinship groups. In the latter part of the archaic period, spanning the fifth and sixth centuries, religion gradually lost its power in politics and society, to be superseded by secular authority as the basis of political power.

A. Unification by Queen Himiko and Emperor Sujin
ca. 250 B.C. to the Second Century A.D.

1. Unification by Queen Himiko

Until the second or third century B.C., the people of the Neolithic age in Japan used stone implements and Jōmon-type earthenware. Then Bronze Age culture was imported from the Asian continent in the second or third century B.C. At roughly the same time, Yayoi-type earthenware appeared in and around Kyushu, and paddy cultivation of rice was begun for the first time. Yayoi earthenware developed under Korean influence and spread gradually to the east where it eventually superseded Jōmon ware as utensils for everyday use. Wet rice cultivation also spread throughout the country from Kyushu, and people living in high, dry areas moved down into lower, moister areas to cultivate the alluvial soil. As they adjusted to a settled way of life, they began to regard each other as kinsmen and formed blood-related lineage groups called *uji*. The area under the rule of one *uji* or a small federation of *uji* was called a *kuni*, or state.

The influx of bronze-age culture provides evidence of a confrontation between two distinct religiocultural spheres. One, centered in northern Kyushu, was characterized by the use of bronze swords or halberds as religious implements; the other, located in and around the Kinai area (today's Nara–Kyoto), was distinguished by the use of *dōtaku* (bell-shaped bronze objects) in religious ceremonies. While these two spheres were delineated in terms of religious and cultural boundaries, presumably they were units of some political significance as well.

The *Han-shu Tili-chih* (Geographical Treatise of the Han History) and *Wei-chih Wojen-ch'uan* (Account of the Japanese in the Wei History)* offer contemporary Chinese accounts of Japan in

* The *History of the Former Han Dynasty* (*Han-shu*) was compiled in the first century A.D., and the *Wa History* (*Wei-chih*), in the third.

that era. Another useful reference is the *Hou-han-shu Wo-ch'uan* (Account of the Japanese in the Later Han History), although this source was not compiled until the fifth century. According to these materials, the two cultural spheres fought each other constantly until both submitted to the rule of Queen Himiko of the Yamatai* state toward the end of the second or beginning of the third century. It is recorded that twenty-eight states pledged fealty to Yamatai. These did not include the states east of the Kinai region, however, which remained independent.

Since the Edo era (1603–1868), scholars have debated whether Yamatai was located in Kyushu or in the Kinai region. According to the *Wei-chih Wojen-ch'uan*, there existed a state of Wa, whose capital was in Yamatai. To get there from northern Kyushu, it was necessary to pass through five thousand *li* of winding sea routes among the islands. If, as I believe, one *li* was equal to about 0.068 miles (0.11 km), five thousand *li* would be a distance of roughly 340 miles (550 km). Even allowing for errors in calculating these distances, the only waterway of that length in the area is the Inland Sea (*Seto Naikai*). From this evidence alone, it seems clear that Yamatai was located at the opposite end of the Inland Sea from Kyushu, *i.e.*, in the Yamato area, today's Nara region.

If our reasoning here is correct, then Himiko's state of Wa would appear to have been a fusion of northern Kyushu and the Kinai area under her rule. The Japanese word for "unify" at that time was *suburu*, which originally meant "to hold gems securely by passing a string through holes in them." The gems represented the various *uji*, and Yamatai itself was a big gem. A string was passed through the gems and they were held tightly, or unified, by Himiko. In old Japanese, the emperor was called *suberagi* or *suberogi*, meaning the "lord who unifies" (*suburu kimi*). As we shall subsequently explain, he held this title as the heir to Himiko, the original "unifier." A state held together in that way might be called a kind of "unified nation" (*tōgō kokka*), and since Yamatai's components were *uji* groups (*ujizoku*), it seems appropriate to refer to it as a "nation of *uji* groups held together" (*ujizoku teki tōgō kokka*).

* It is likely that the characters spelling out "Yamatai" were in fact pronounced "Yamato" at the time, but it is now the practice to pronounce them "Yamatai" to distinguish this name from the "Yamato" of the Kinai area.

We have already noted that archaic society was theoretically ruled by the gods. However, since they themselves could not rule directly, they exercised their powers through human agents. Gods entered human bodies, and men thus possessed revealed the divine will through their words. Since the god's will was absolute, the person through whom it was transmitted could wield absolute power over *uji* members and their slaves. Only the designated leader of the *uji*, called the *uji-no-kami*, could perceive the divine will. The tutelary god of an *uji* was called its *ujigami*. Only the *uji* chieftain had the right to worship (*matsuru*) this god and convey (*noru*) the divine will. The chieftain controlled his *uji* by virtue of this mystic authority. In the *Wei-chih Wojen-ch'uan* we rad that "Himiko was versed in the way of the spirits and could bewitch the people," suggesting the mystic attributes of the *uji* leader. Female government was not unusual in archaic times, as may be surmised from the fact that Amaterasu-ōmikami, said to be the progenitor of the imperial family, was in fact a goddess. *Matsuri* (worship) actually meant "serving the gods and knowing their will." Later the word came to imply the ritual associated with this service. The words for "governing the state" were *shiroshimesu* and *shirasu*, both of which are reverential forms of the verb *shiru*, "to know." As these words indicate, one could govern the state only by "knowing" the will of the gods. It often happens in Japanese that the word denoting cause comes to describe the result as well. At any rate, the root of the normative power of law lay in religious authority, and at that time the two were not yet distinct spheres.

We have seen that there were two terms which could denote "control" in archaic times, *shiru* ("to know") and *suburu* ("to hold together or unify"). While the two are generally understood to be interchangeable, *shiru* strictly speaking implied control held by the *uji* members and their servants through their religious powers. On the other hand, *suburu* technically referred to the way in which one *uji* controlled another. Although *suburu* also had religious connotations, the principal element in one *uji*'s control over another was mainly military power.

It might be added that Himiko confined herself to the inner recesses of the court after becoming the ruler of Wa, and very few people enjoyed access to her. Her brother apparently took charge of the mundane affairs of state, for the *Wei-chih* tells us that "she had a brother who assisted her in ruling the state." In other words, although Himiko was the source of the right to rule, she herself did not actually govern. Himiko's situation was not unique; it reflected, in fact, the general practice of the time among *uji* chieftains. It set a precedent, however, that became the origin of the tradition that the emperor of Japan does not personally run the government.

2. Unification by Emperor Sujin

Himiko died sometime in the middle of the third century and was succeeded by a female member of her clan, Toyo. Yamatai was able to rise to a preeminent position among the states of Wa because of the assistance it received from the Wei dynasty in China. After the collapse of the Han dynasty, the three states of Wei, Wu, and Shu stood confronting one another. Shu was located in the west, and Wu held sway in the south. Wei occupied the northeast and controlled southern Korea. Koguryo, whose rule extended from northern Korea into Manchuria, allied itself with Wu. To counter this alliance, Wei was obliged to join hands with Japan, and provided Yamatai with the military and political assistance required to establish hegemony over twenty-eight other states. However, Wei was conquered by the Western Ch'in in A.D. 265, and the influence of Toyo's Yamatai probably declined with the termination of support from her continental ally. Yamatai was soon attacked by the ruler of a growing state in northern Kyushu, who successfully took over Toyo's political power without prolonged hostilities. In the earliest official Japanese sources, the *Nihon shoki* and *Kojiki*, which were compiled in the eighth century, this ruler is identified as Sujin, the tenth emperor of Japan.

According to the *Nihon shoki* and *Kojiki*, the first emperor was Jinmu, who launched an expedition eastward from Kyushu and assumed the throne in the year 660 B.C. However, scholars now believe that the date 660 B.C. was calculated on the basis of ancient Chinese calendar lore introduced to Japan in the fifth or sixth century. Chroniclers of that era simply assumed that a great upheaval had taken place in Japan 1260 years prior to the ninth year of Empress Suiko's reign (*i.e.*, 600 A.D.), and that the first emperor was enthroned in that year. That there was such an eastward expedition is not to be doubted, but it was led by Sujin, not Jinmu. In fact, Sujin was the first emperor of Japan; he, as well as Jinmu, is cited in the aforementioned Japanese chronicles as "the first emperor ruling the state" (*hatsukuni-shirasu-sumeramikoto*). These theories are corroborated by Sujin's presumed date of death (A.D. 318) and by the fact that he had a palace in the area of Himiko's "Yamato" (near Mount Miwa in present-day Nara Prefecture). Further evidence that Sujin launched an eastward expedition from northern Kyushu is suggested by the fact that armed expeditions to Kyushu led by the twelfth and fourteenth emperors (Keikō and Chūai) completely ignored the northern part of the island. Since northern Kyushu had already been subjugated by Sujin before his departure eastward, the two later emperors' attention could be focused exclusively on the southeast part of the island.

Toyosuki-iri-hime-no-mikoto, said to be Sujin's daughter, was actually the defeated Toyo, to whom the emperor accorded the rank of imperial princess. Yamato-totohi-momoso-hime-no-mikoto, said to be the emperor's aunt, who helped him by communing with the gods, was in all probability the deceased Himiko. In any case, Sujin enshrined the sacred mirror (one of the imperial family's three sacred treasures) in his palace as a symbol of his divine ancestor Amaterasu-ōmikami (the sun goddess). Later, however, he transferred the mirror to the Kasanui-mura in Yamato. This act may be interpreted as evidence that Sujin wished to have Amaterasu-ōmikami revered not only as the tutelary god of the imperial house but as the tutelary god of all other *uji* as well. When the emperor achieved control (*suburu*) over the other *uji* by military force, his power was only relative; but when it was sanctioned by "knowing" the divine will of the great tutelary god of all *uji*, his control (*shiru*) became rooted in divine authority and his authority became absolute.

It is believed that Sujin's approach to imperial authority was adopted by each succeeding emperor and became traditional imperial policy. The eleventh emperor (Suinin)'s daughter, Yamato-hime-no-mikoto, carried the sacred mirror through Ōmi and Mino to the bank of the Isuzu River in Ise where she installed it permanently. The people of Yamato saw the sun rise over the horizon of Ise in the east, and Ise was therefore deemed the most suitable site for the mirror. The legendary "first emperor" Jinmu, too, reputedly paid homage to the east and the sun goddess by starting his expedition from Hyūga (meaning "facing the sun") in eastern Kyushu.

B. Formation of the *Amenoshita-shiroshimesu-sumeramikoto*
Middle Archaic Period, Third and Fourth Centuries

1. Amenoshita-shiroshimesu-sumeramikoto

As the throne moved from northern Kyushu to Yamato, the San'yō area between these points was subjugated by Kibitsuhiko-no-mikoto under Emperor Sujin's orders. The Kumaso of southern Kyushu were attacked subsequently by expeditions of the twelfth emperor, Keikō, but they resisted the imperial forces tenaciously. Another force was dispatched by the fourteenth emperor, Chūai, but it was diverted to attach southern Korea from northern Kyushu in accordance with a divine oracle transmitted to Chūai's wife, Empress Jingū. The chronicles report that the empress herself led the invading armies, but some doubt exists as to whether she was a real person or a creation of later historians. It is certain, at any rate, that Japan did invade Korea on several occasions around A.D. 400. That fact is borne out by an inscription on a monument to the monarch of the kingdom of Koguryo; the monument, incidentally, still stands in southern Manchuria. As a result of these expeditions, large-scale importation of Chinese culture to Japan from Korea began. The important point from the viewpoint of political development, however, is that within one hundred years of Emperor Sujin's reign, Japan's rulers had acquired sufficient financial and military strength to send troops across the sea into a foreign land.

Thus, the emperors succeeded ultimately in establishing control (*suburu*) over the other *uji*, which took the form of divinely-informed rule (*shiru*). It was probably from around this time, therefore, that the emperor was first called the "one with the divine sanction to hold the world together" (*amenoshita-shiroshimesu-su-meramikoto*). Since *amenoshita* (the world) referred specifically to Japan, this imposing title actually denoted the emperor as "one with the divine authority to rule Japan." He had developed into a strong political leader, who successfully combined religious authority with political might. If any physical evidence is required to demonstrate in concrete terms the imposing position of the emperor, we need look no further than the huge mausolea housing the graves of Chūai's successors, the emperors Ōjin and Nintoku. Indeed, the majesty of the imperial throne can readily be surmised from the epic proportions of Nintoku's Takatsuka tomb—the largest burial mound in the world.

2. The *Uji*

We know very little about the organization of the *uji* in archaic Japan, but it was undoubtedly a group led by the patriarchal *uji-no-kami*, or *uji* "chieftain." As the leader of the *uji*, the chieftain was responsible for worshiping its tutelary god, supervising the *uji*, adjudicating disputes among *uji* members, and dealing with outsiders. The territory (*kuni*) and people under *uji* control were subject to the direct rule of the chieftain. The emperor's control (*suburu*) was exercised only indirectly, through the local chieftain; as we have noted, that control had acquired a degree of sanctity through his knowledge of the divine will (*shiru*). The chieftain had certain areas of cultivated land marked off to satisfy his personal needs. These areas were known variously as *tadokoro* (cultivated lands) or *nari-dokoro* (productive lands). During this period the symbols of the chieftain's powers (as well as of those of the emperor) were the mirror, sword, and jewel. In summary, religious and civil affairs were fused together in the society of this era. The historical role of religion as the basis for secular political power was clearly manifest, distinguishing the middle part of the archaic period from the periods that followed.

3. Penal Law

That the gods ruled supreme at this time is clear in the area of penal law. The word for "crime" in the vocabulary of the time was *tsumi*, which is said to have connoted "hiding" or "concealment" (*tsutsumi kakusu*). In other words, a *tsumi* was anything which would displease the gods and therefore became necessary to conceal from them. When the gods' displeasure was aroused by a crime, they could only be appeased through the rite of purification (*harae*). *Harae* literally meant "shaking off," or cleansing, the filth attached to one's person as a result of a transgression. In form, the rite required an offering (*harae-tsu-mono*), accompanied by a priestly invocation of the words of *harae* to the gods. *Misogi* (ritual ablution) was another means of purification; it consisted of immersing oneself in water and having the filth washed away by its cleaning power.

One method of divining the veracity of evidence presented at a trial was an ordeal called *kukadachi*. The suspect or witness was obliged to remove a hot stone from boiling water, and his credibility was determined in accordance with whether his hand was injured or not.

C. The State Based on *Uji* and *Kabane*
Early Fifth Century to 603

1. Changes in the Form of Imperial Control

Sometime around the end of the fourth or beginning of the fifth century, Japan established control over part of Korea, and in so doing came into extensive contact with the civilization of the continent. That exposure resulted in increased familiarity with secular Confucianism. In the area of penal law, these new influences led to gradual recognition of the Chinese concept of secular crime and punishment. While the Japanese accepted the validity of this concept in time, there was an initial period of transition with frequent instances when both *harae* ("purification") and secular punishment were required as penance for the same crime.

The rise of secular authority became pronounced in politics as well, curbing the great influence of religious authority that was so pronounced prior to the fifth century. As a result of the diminution of divine authority, the significance of the emperor's "knowing" the will of the gods also decreased. Although it was still common to refer to the emperor's rule as *shiru*, this term now meant "obtaining knowledge" from the reports of imperial officials such as *ōomi* and *ōmuraji*, rather than from the gods. While the emperor continued to be the source of political legitimacy, his activities were confined to receiving administrative reports; the tradition of imperial divorce from actual political leadership was maintained, as it had been since Himiko's era. As secularization progressed, the term *matsurigoto* no longer referred to the emperor's serving the gods, but came to describe the function of officials serving the emperor and governing the country.

There was a variety of official posts (*tsukasa*) in the imperial administration; late in the archaic period holders of these posts (*tsukasa-bito*) were considered to exercise their powers and duties as a trust from the throne. Only those with hereditary "titles" (*kabane*) could fill a post, and hence the right to hold positions also tended to become hereditary. Three posts commonly held by central government officials were *omi, muraji,* and *tomo-no-miyatsuko*.* *Omi* and *muraji* were originally hereditary titles, but later they became synonymous with specific posts. Naturally not all title holders actually received official appointments. *Kabane* only qualified their holders to hold posts; they did not make appointment automatic.

During this era, there were two subordinate classes attached to the *uji*: *kakibe* and *nuhi*. The *kakibe* were a class of laborers created and owned by *uji* chieftains; their function was to cultivate his lands, make weapons, and provide other essentials. (*Kaki* means "organize" while *be* connotes "squad" or "group.") The *nuhi* belonged to the *ie* ("house"), a suborganization of the *uji*, and they were considered property that could be traded or given away. *Kakibe* were attached to the court in great numbers and were generally called *shinajina-no-tomo* or *shinabe* when attached to the imperial household. Included among the latter were several types of *be* not found in ordinary *uji*. The officials responsible for managing these *shinabe* or *shinajina-no-tomo* were called *tomo-no-miyatsuko*.

The court derived revenue from two kinds of taxation, according to old historical chronicles. The *mitsugi* tax corresponded to the *chō* tax of a later era, on the produce of each area, and the *edachi* tax was analogous to the later *eki* levy on labor. They were evidently collected from the *uji* by the court as necessity dictated. In addition, a *tachikara* tax, similar to the later *so* property tax, was collected from *miyake* and *miagata*, districts under direct control of the court. No *tachikara* tax was directly levied on territories controlled by the other *uji*.

* "*Omi*" and "*muraji*" designated participants in the national government. "*Tomo-no-miyatsuko*" had the duty of managing groups of people (*tomo*) organized by the court to provide for its needs.

The emperor played a pivotal role in Japan's relations with outside powers and in legitimizing the exercise of political power at home by one or another of a number of competing groups. Looking first at his role in foreign relations, we see that from early in the fifth century to early in the sixth, Japanese emperors sent messengers and tribute to the successive dynasties of the southern court in China. In turn, they received appointments from the Chinese emperor to serve as local governors in Korea and Japan. Obviously Japan's relationship with China was not that of an equal. However, Japan lost its only foothold on the continent when Mimana, long a Japanese base at the southern end of the Korean peninsula, was overrun by the kingdom of Silla in 562.

At home, the emperor's capital moved from the Mount Miwa area southwest to Asuka, and for brief periods it was, for the purpose of continental relations, located in Settsu and Kawachi. (See the map of the Kinai region on p. 15.) In consonance with the tradition of indirect rule, the local leaders of Asuka were appointed to important posts and took charge of the government. At first the Katsuragi *shi* (*uji*) held the most powerful appointments, but power soon shifted to the Ōtomo. Later the Mononobe and Soga *shi* became the chief competitors, and when the forces of the former were defeated, the Soga achieved a monopoly on political power. It is noteworthy that all of these *uji* (except the Mononobe) became powerful at court by marrying their daughters to the emperors.

Some have theorized that new dynasties were actually established under Emperor Ōjin and again under Emperor Keitai. Others hold that Emperor Sujin was really a member of a race of mounted warriors who came from the continent to conquer the old dynasty early in the fourth century. None of these theories, however, is supported by strong evidence.

2. Territories under Direct Imperial Control

Land was classified according to whether it was under direct rule of the emperor or whether it was in areas ruled by other *uji* chieftains (*kuni*). Some imperial lands were probably presented to the throne by other chieftains; the rest were acquired as a result of military conquest. In areas directly ruled by the emperor, the court appointed governors called *kuni-no-miyatsuko*. Often the local chieftain was nominated for this post after he acknowledged the emperor's authority over him. Hence, the *kuni-no-miyatsuko* post retained some of the religious character of the former *uji* chieftain's position. Since many of the *kuni-no-miyatsuko* were later nominated to serve as local governors in the secular *ritsuryō* system of administration, we may surmise that the *kuni* corresponded in size to the later *kōri* (*gun*) administrative unit. The term *kuni* was eventually applied not only to *uji* lands but to administrative subdivisions of the emperor's own territory. Within the *kuni*, one smaller administrative unit was the *kōri*, governed by officials called *inagi*. Another unit was the *agata*, which originally referred to land owned by the court and supervised by officials called *agata-nushi*. Like the *kuni*, however, the term *agata* eventually came to denote a unit of local administration. Apart from these units, village-like units called *sato, mura,* and *fure* had long existed and were governed by *mura-kimi, mura-obito,* etc.

3. Functions of the Kabane and Uji

It is believed that the Japanese experience in administering part of Korea stimulated consciousness of the concept of "state" in Japan. This consciousness presumably strengthened the political and economic coherence of the imperial government. The growth of the *kabane* system was one manifestation of this trend. Originally, the *kabane* appears to have been a term of respect used privately by *uji* members in referring to their chieftains. The imperial court later used the term as a kind of title denoting the respective positions of the chieftains in the imperial state. If, as is theorized, the word *kabane* originated in Korea in Silla's *koppin* system, the term must date from after the foundation of the state of Silla in the middle of the fourth century. Since it was considered a great honor to receive official posts, chieftains were often referred to deferentially by the names of their posts, and thus the word describing the post became a respectful name, or title (*kabane*). Some titles were: *kimi, wake, omi, muraji, tomo-no-miyatsuko, obito, atae, kuni-no-miyatsuko, inagi, agata-nushi,* and *suguri*. Once *kabane* had become a part of the system of state, the court frequently conferred *kabane* on *uji* in recognition of meritorious service. Promotions and demotions also occurred, and, on occasion, *uji* were stripped of their *kabane*.

Meanwhile, the authority of the tutelary god (*ujigami*) in each *uji* disappeared, and the status of the *uji* chieftain became dependent on the emperor. *Uji* were judged according to whether or not they were properly fulfilling their obligations (*waza*) to the emperor. For example, two *uji*—the Ōtomo and the Kume—were assigned the task of guarding the court, while the duty of the Nakatomi and Inbe *uji* was to perform the religious ceremonies of the court. Each *uji* chieftain led his *uji* in the performance of its appointed *waza* for the emperor. When performing those duties, the *uji* was called a *tomo*, its chieftain was referred to as the *tomo-no-miyatsuko*, and *uji* members were regarded as *tomo-no-o*. In time, the chieftain's supreme concern revolved around whether his *uji* was duly performing its *waza* for the court. The responsibility for performing the *uji*'s duty was the central element in the legacy inherited by successive chieftains. Later, when *uji* broke down into *ie* (houses), "house duties" (*ie no waza,* or *kagyō*)) became the basic concept of inheritance. From the latter part of the archaic period until the enactment of the Meiji Civil Code in 1898, the inheritance of *waza* in one form or another was, I believe, the central concept of inheritance itself.

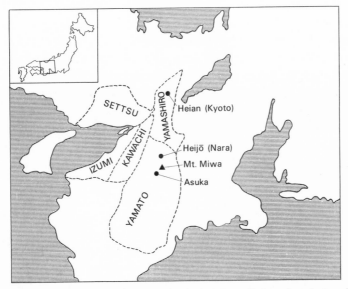

The Kinai region and sites of importance during the archaic and ancient periods. The five "home provinces" are indicated as well as the various locations of the emperor's court.

CHAPTER 2

THE TAIKA REFORM AND FORMATION OF THE *RITSURYŌ*-STYLE UNIFIED STATE

Jōsei, or Ancient Period, 603–967

The *ritsuryō* system of government was introduced into Japan from China during the ancient period (603–967). By the latter part of the archaic period, law and religion had evolved into almost completely distinct spheres. The secular *ritsuryō* system therefore took root with comparative ease. Indeed, the separation of law and religion was a central characteristic of this period.

Ritsu and *ryō* were legal codes. The century in which they took root in Japan (603–702) constitutes the first part of the ancient period. It was a century of internal turbulence and upheaval, symbolized by Prince Shōtoku's new regime, the Taika Reform, and the Jinshin War. In contrast, the following century (702–810) saw the unrest subside as the *ritsuryō* system reached its peak of effectiveness. The personal rule of the emperor (*tennō shinsei*) over the whole nation was now established for the first time. The last years of the ancient period (from 810 to 967) were a time of transition, in which the *ritsuryō* system was gradually undermined. The collapse of the imported *ritsuryō* system was accompanied by partial reversion to the native traditions of the archaic period.

A. The Taika Reform (603–702)

1. Prince Shōtoku's New Government

At the end of the archaic period the leaders of the Soga *shi* (*uji*)

17

were so inflated with power that they assassinated Emperor Sushun. Empress Suiko succeeded Sushun to the throne. In the following year (593), she designated her nephew, Prince Umayado (later called Prince Shōtoku), as crown prince and entrusted him with control of the government. At that time, Soga no Umako held responsibility for the government as chief minister (ōomi). Hence, Umayado's elevation to the position of crown prince with full control of the government raised him to a position of importance equal to that of Umako. It is usually stated, in fact, that Umayado was made prince regent (sesshō), although his position was somewhat more analogous to the kanpaku (chief imperial advisor) post of later years.

In the twelfth month of 603, a twelve-tier system of court ranks was established. Hitherto the key prerequisite for obtaining official posts at court had been a kabane obtained through inheritance. Under the new system, however, ranks were bestowed in consideration of the recipient's merit and ability, rather than his patrimony. Not surprisingly, beneficiaries of the kabane system resisted the new system of court ranks, and the issue was not settled until the enactment a century later, in 701, of the Taihō code, which established the primacy of the court ranking system. (This rivalry over rankings, in fact, can be said to characterize the first half of the ancient period.) However, it should be noted that the twelve-tier system was not meant to destroy kabane. Its purport was rather to place the right of conferring ranks squarely with the court. Its significance lay in the emphasis placed on the emperor as sovereign power. In 604, one year after the rank system was created, Prince Shōtoku promulgated a seventeen-article constitution which was designed in part to emphasize the same point. The document was not actually a constitution in the modern sense of the word, but rather a set of moral precepts for the officials of state and for the people. Article twelve stressed that "no state has two sovereigns, and no people have two masters." In this way, Prince Shōtoku insisted that there was no source of political authority and legitimacy other than the imperial throne.

2. The Taika Reform

Soga no Umako kept his peace while Prince Shōtoku was alive, but after the crown prince's death in 622, the Soga were again able to wield power unchecked, acting as if they were the sovereign power. Predictably, a movement centered around the court arose in an attempt to destroy the Soga.

In the sixth month of 645, Prince Naka no Ōe, Nakatomi no Kamatari, and others succeeded in shattering Soga power, ending an era in which the state seemed to have had two sovereigns. Nevertheless, *uji* chieftains continued to maintain control in areas outside territory directly controlled by the emperor. The T'ang dynasty was then in the process of extending its borders in many directions, and the powerful Korean state of Silla also loomed as a threat to Japan. In order to deter invasions from either state, Japan's strength had to be bolstered; that meant reforming its own institutions. It was in this context that the Taika Reform was carried out. The model was provided by the T'ang *ritsuryō* system.

Reform began with the confiscation of all land and people held officially by *uji* chieftains. Historians usually date this confiscation from the imperial rescript on reform issued in 646, but the rescript's first article provided only for expropriation of cultivated lands owned by the emperor and influential groups in order to establish state authority over cultivated land and to implement a land re-distribution program (*handen shūju hō*, provided for in Article Three of the same rescript). It had nothing to do with expropriating lands and people held officially by the *uji* chieftains. In my view, the confiscation of privately owned land and people took place in 645, immediately after the Soga were destroyed. The oath taken in the sixth month of that year under the great *tsuki* (pandanus) tree af-firmed that only one government should exist under one ruler (*kimi*). Previously, while the emperor was referred to as *ōkimi* (great *kimi*), *uji* chieftains were also called *kimi*. The purport of the oath was to declare that only the government of the *ōkimi* (the emperor) was legitimate, and that the public authority of the *uji* chieftains was no longer recognized. The entire country now came under the direct administration of the court, and was converted from a nation of loosely tied groups (*tōgō kokka*) into a tightly unified and integrated centralized state (*tōitsu kokka*) on the Chinese model. This trans-formation was the most remarkable development since the unifi-cation of the *uji* by the emperor Sujin. It was celebrated by the adoption for the first time of a commemorative name (*nengō*) for the era; the name selected, Taika ("great metamorphosis"), was probably intended to glorify the event.

After the court declared the expropriation of the land held officially by the chieftains in 645, it instituted measures to implement the declaration. On the first day of 646, the four-article imperial reform edict was promulgated at the Nagara-Toyosaki palace in the new capital of Settsu (present-day Osaka). The four articles constituted a declaration of the new policies of the government. The first, as noted earlier, provided for expropriation of cultivated fields owned by the emperor and influential groups and the liberation of men enslaved to them. Article Two specified three kinds of local administrative units, *kuni, kōri* (or *gun*), and *sato* (*ri* or *gō*), and three kinds of officials, *kokushi* (*kuni no tsukasa*), *gunji* (*kōri no tsukasa*), and *richo* (*gōchō* or *sato-osa*), to govern them. Since the entire country was placed under direct control of the emperor's government, a new system of local administration was required. Article Three identified its basic components: household registers (*koseki*), a law for redistributing land (*handen shūju hō*), annual financial reports (*keichō*), and land taxation (*sō*). House registers had been drawn up earlier in some areas under direct imperial control; now that the emperor's control was to extend nationwide, the registration system was also established among all people under his rule. Administrators would require that registers be drawn up to maintain official records on all the people and to carry out land redistribution (*handen shūju hō*). This land redistribution, which will be discussed in greater detail, had social objectives and can therefore be regarded as Japan's first agrarian reform. Annual financial reports (*keichō*) were to serve as a basis for *chō* and *yō* produce and labor taxes. Article Four concerned taxation and provided regulations for *chō* and *yō*.

Although the 646 reform edict contained no special stipulations regarding the structure of a central government, such regulations were soon issued. In 649, a system of "eight ministries and one hundred official posts" (*hasshō hyakkan*) was decreed, providing suitable dignity and majesty for the new state organization.

3. Rule by the Crown Prince

As crown prince (*kōtaishi*), Shōtoku held the reins of government together with the chief minister, Soga no Umako. This initiated a new political form, in which the crown prince was vested with sovereign power. We have previously noted that the traditional divorce of the emperor from the governing process apparently began around Himiko's time. By the end of the archaic period, however, Japanese were familiar with the Chinese notion of direct imperial rule. They were able to harmonize this concept with their own prevailing political traditions by instituting direct rule by the crown prince rather than by the emperor himself. Hence, it was Crown Prince Naka no Ōe who carried out the Taika Reform, while Emperor Kōtoku remained aloof from the affairs of state.

Naka no Ōe was also responsible for governing as crown prince under Kōtoku's successor, Empress Saimei. In 668, he himself assumed the throne as Emperor Tenji. Tenji's son was then too young to be designated crown prince, so the emperor named his own younger brother, Prince Ōama, as "brother imperial" (*kō-taitei*) in charge of running the government. In 671, the emperor appointed Prince Ōtomo as prime minister (*daijōdaijin*) and the two princes shared the responsibility of governing the realm. Prince Ōama was displeased by this development, and after the emperor died, he and Ōtomo began a feud which grew into the Jinshin War of 672. Ultimately, Ōtomo was defeated and Ōama ascended to the throne as Emperor Tenmu. His son was also too young to be named crown prince, and the responsibilities of government consequently devolved upon the empress. She cooperated with the emperor in governing until the young crown prince was sufficiently mature to assume control.

4. Ōmi ryō and Tenmu ryō

The legal code drawn up under Emperor Tenji is called the *Ōmi ryō*. The household registers compiled according to this code in 670 still showed strong regard for the old *uji* and *kabane*. Indeed, the *Ōmi ryō* in its entirety seems to have been remarkably conservative. One might expect that Tenji, who had carried out the Taika Reform as crown prince, would be a progressive emperor, but during the time he governed under Empress Saimei, the troops he sent to Korea were repulsed. Weakened politically by this defeat, he was obliged to follow conservative policies thereafter in order to gain the support of other influential groups.

Emperor Tenmu, who acceded to the throne against the wishes

of the late Emperor Tenji, was eager to promote men of ability, and he drew up a code known as the *Tenmu ryō* with this objective in mind. However, opposition from a number of influential groups obstructed its implementation. Finally, a new system of eight *kabane* was decreed in order to downgrade the prestige of the old *kabane*. The *Tenmu ryō* was enforced in 689, after Tenmu's consort, Empress Jitō, formally succeeded to the position of her deceased husband.

B. The Emperor-centered *Ritsuryō* Integrated State
Nara era, 702–810

1. The Emperor

Empress Jitō was succeeded on the throne by Monmu, Tenmu's grandson. In 701, Monmu issued the Taihō code, providing the final component of *ritsuryō*-style government. *Ritsuryō* administration sought to cultivate popular morality and enable the people to become ideal Confucian citizens (a concept which will be discussed in detail later). Officials were given the task of edifying the populace and were themselves to be guided by the emperor. The model of imperial conduct held up by Japanese emperors running a Chinese-style bureaucratic system was also Chinese. The codes borrowed the Chinese word for emperor (*kōtei*) to refer to the Japanese sovereign (*tennō*), suggesting that the *tennō* concept had evolved to denote a despotic, Chinese-type sovereign who personally looked after the affairs of state.

A capital was built in Nara, modeled on the T'ang imperial capital city of Chang-an, although Nara, unlike Chang-an, was not surrounded by a high wall. The time when Nara served as the capital of Japan is usually called the Nara period (710–784), but I have used "Nara era" more loosely to include a number of years before and after the capital was established there.

2. Ritsuryō Kyakushiki

The Taihō code (*Taihō ritsuryō*) was formally issued at Fujiwara-kyō (capital 694–710). A penal code (*ritsu*) apparently had been drafted earlier under Emperor Tenmu, but it was probably not completed. The Taihō code was the first legal code in Japan, then, containing both penal (*ritsu*) and administrative (*ryō*) law. It remained in force until 757, when it was supplanted by the Yōrō code. Since the Taihō code did not, as a unit, survive the ravages of time and history, this new one, actually compiled as early as 718, is the oldest extant legal code.

The idea of an exhaustive system of enacted law, made up of *ritsuryō* and *kyakushiki*, dates from the Sui and T'ang classification of written Chinese dynastic laws. Both *ritsu* and *ryō* were issued as codes, *ritsu* relating to the chastisement of evil and *ryō* related to the promotion of righteousness. Together they were meant to enlighten and civilize men, guiding them toward the high moral ideals of Confucianism. When the codes were introduced in Japan, their architects transplanted the T'ang system of *ritsu* virtually intact. The only revisions involved reducing penalties by a degree or two. On the other hand, the emperor's legal officers scaled the *ryō* down and amended them to meet Japan's particular needs. Some new rules were also established after careful consideration.

As social conditions and requirements changed, further amendment of the *ritsu* and *ryō* became desirable. Individual amendments to the *ritsu* and *ryō* were called *kyaku*, and minor regulations dealing with implementation of the codes were classified as *shiki*. The lawmakers no doubt believed that their written law, combining *ritsuryō* and *kyakushiki*, could regulate all important affairs of state. In reality, however, they could not prevent the development of certain administrative practices which contradicted the law. These practices were called *toki no gyōji* ("contemporary practice") or, more simply, *gyōji* ("exceptions in practice").

The science of law did not flourish in Japan before the Meiji era. The Nara and Heian eras were exceptional in that many legal scholars and new schools of thought emerged, but legal science at that stage of history did not develop much beyond commentaries on terminology.

3. The Daijōkan* System

The *ryō* provided for a central government comprised of two offices (*daijōkan* and *jingikan*), eight ministries (*shō*), and one police agency, or "officials' court" (*danjōdai*). The *daijōkan* was the

* "*Daijōkan*" is the more authentic pronounciation of this central office, but by the Meiji period, the pronounciation "*Dajōkan*" had become customary.

central office of the government, while the *jingikan* was responsible for Shintō rites. The three ministries of the T'ang government were adopted and used in Japan. In the Chinese bureaucracy the *chungshu-sheng* handled the drafting of imperial rescripts; the *menhsia-sheng* examined the rescripts and submitted them to the emperor, and the *shangshu-sheng* were the executors of the rescripts. One of the system's defects, however, was that the *chungshu-sheng* became too powerful, and an administrative balance of power could not be maintained. To right this imbalance the Japanese combined their versions of the *menhsia-sheng* and *shangshu-sheng* into the *daijōkan*, leaving the *chungshu-sheng* (or *nakatsukasa-shō*, as it became in Japan) as just one of eight ministries. The *daijōkan* had two leading officials, the *sadaijin* (minister of the left) and the *udaijin* (minister of the right); the status of the former was superior to that of the latter. The highest *daijōkan* minister—the *daijōdaijin*—was in fact an advisor to the emperor without specific duties, and the post ordinarily remained unfilled. The eight ministries responsible for various areas of government were placed under the *daijōkan*. Finally, the office that supervised official conduct was *danjōdai*, modeled after the T'ang *yushih-t'ai*. An imperial guard was created with five divisions to protect the imperial palace, serve as honor guards, and patrol the capital city.

Each government office in the *ryō* system had four grades of regular officials: *kami* (chief), *suke* (vice-chief), *jō* (discipline officer), and *sakan* (clerks). Moreover, one had to possess a "corresponding court rank" in order to receive appointment to any official post. One could acquire court rank by passing state examinations or receive a rank called "grace rank" (*on'i*) by virtue of the rank held by one's father or grandfather. Passing the state examination, however, only opened the way to low-ranking posts; all higher offices were occupied by the sons and grandsons of officials with high court rank, who obtained it by virtue of their patrimonies. Although the *ritsuryō* government abolished the *kabane* system and in theory opened the way for the advance of able men through the system of court ranks and state examinations, these innovations were increasingly circumvented. Once an influential family reached high position, there was always a danger that it would monopolize the high posts. Indeed, the Fujiwara subsequently availed themselves of this system to seize all important court posts.

4. The Local Administrative System

The local administrative system outlined in the Taika Reform, and amplified later in the *ryō*, divided the country into three types of administrative units, *kuni, kōri*, and *sato* (fifty-household groups), governed respectively by *kokushi, gunji*, and *richō*. The *kokushi* were responsible for civil government and justice in their *kuni*. They were dispatched by the central government to serve a fixed term of office locally, and then replaced. Their most important duty was to implement the policies of moral enlightenment conceived by the central government. There were four levels within the *kokushi* category: *kami, suke, jo*, and *sakau*; at times the term *kokushi* referred only to the highest of the four, the "governor" or *kami*. After 757 it became the practice for *kokushi* to receive a percentage of any funds (of rice) left over from the amounts allocated for official business. Such surpluses were called *kugetō*, and when added to a *kokushi's* orginal salary they made his income very large indeed. Some *kokushi* managed to procure a share of *kugetō* without even going to their local posts. Those who remained in the capital were euphemistically called *yōju-kokushi* (*"kokushi* stationed afar"). The local offices of these absentee *kokushi* were called *rusudokoro* (absentee offices), and officials serving there were known as *zaichō kanjin* (officials who are actually in the office). High-ranking court officials were not permitted to hold the lower post of *kokushi* because their ranks limited them to more exalted positions. Because they wished to share in the allocation of *kugetō*, however, they obtained the right to nominate men for *kokushi* posts and as patrons claimed their nominees' *kugetō* shares. This system of supplementing the wealth of high-ranking court officials was called *nenkan* (yearly office), because they had the opportunity to make recommendations every year or at fixed intervals of two or more years.

Gunji were the most important of the *kokushi's* local subordinates; they exercised administrative and judicial authority at the *gun* level. *Gunji*, particularly those with the high official status of *kami* or *suke*, were appointed from among the leading families of the *gun*. In contrast to the *kokushi*, *gunji* held their appointments for life.

Just as high posts in the capital were monopolized by hereditary nobility through "grace rank," local *gunji* positions soon came under the exclusive control of certain prominent families in each area. The widely heralded system of promotions based on talent was significant only at the low levels of the bureaucracy, not at the *gunji* level. The growth of hereditary control over access to the *gunji* post was highly significant, for it became one of the factors responsible for the emergence of the *bushi* (warrior class) in the Middle Ages (*chūsei*).

The *gun* unit was composed of *sato* (or *ri*), each of which consisted of fifty households (*he* or *ko*). *Richō* (*ri* headmen) were appointed from among the honest and able-bodied peasants of the *ri*. The *ko* was an administrative unit containing a "head" (*ko-chō* or *he-nushi*) and "members" (*ko-ko*), and all were officially listed in the household registers. Intermediate between the *ri* and *ko* was an organ called *go-ho*; it was composed of *ko-chō* from five neighboring *ko*, and was designed to subject each of them to the surveillance of the others.

The standard administrative system was not used in the capital city, which had had its own unique system since the Taika Reform. It was bifurcated into a "left city" and a "right city" by a street (*suzaku ōji*) running from north to south. Each "city" had its own mayor, the *sakyō-shiki* ("mayor of the left city") and *ukyōshiki* ("mayor of the right city"). Another exception to the standard system of local administration was the establishment of a special superintendency (*dazaifu*) over the nine *kuni* and two islands (Tsushima and Iki) of the Kyushu area. This office was created in view of Kyushu's vital importance in internal politics and foreign relations.

Local militia were recruited by the conscription of about one-third of those in each *kuni* who were of eligible age. One unit was established for about every four *gun*, and soldiers were required to pay for their own weapons and food.

5. Land Redistribution and Taxation

a) Land Redistribution Law and Household Registration. Both the land redistribution law (*handen shūju hō*) and the household registration system were instituted generally during the Taika Reform. The former was modeled on the T'ang *chuntien-fa* ("equal field law"), which was created by the Northern Wei of the "Northern

Court" as a means of local recovery from barbarian invasions. Japan's problems were not occasioned by foreign invasion or any need to restore agrarian productivity; they derived from a desire to institute a measure of equality in land ownership. Until the Taika Reform was instituted, land was held almost exclusively by large-scale landowners. Few ordinary peasants owned land, surviving instead as cultivators on land owned by the big landlords. The object of the land redistribution law in Japan was to remedy this evil by allowing the common people to have a share of land and by assuring them a minimum standard of living. The measure therefore had greater social meaning than the Chinese "equal field law'" which allocated fields even to farm oxen while ignoring infants incapable of land cultivation. Moreover, the Chinese system required the elderly to surrender half or all of their fields, while women, whose work was considered to be weaving and the like, were denied the right to receive land. The systems in the two countries had quite different objectives. In Japan, men and women were both entitled to land after reaching their sixth year, and this land was not confiscated in old age. The amount of land granted (*kubunden*) was two *tan* (about six-tenths of an acre) for men, and two-thirds of a man's share for a woman. Reapportionments took place only every six years, so those not yet six years old had to wait until the next apportionment year to receive their land. Fields granted to a person remained his until his death.

Eligibility to receive land was determined on the basis of household registers; the registers were thus updated and recompiled every sixth year. At the same time, they served to record the status and family relations of individuals, and kept the records clear on *uji* membership and possession of *kabane*. Vagrants and wanderers could also be controlled this way.

b) *Taxation*. There were three T'ang-style taxes sanctioned by the *ryō* system. *So* was a yield tax levied on crops from fields designated as taxable (*yusoden*). (Nontaxable land under cultivation was called *fu-yusoden*.) The most important type of *yusoden* was *kubunden*. The *so* tax amounted to around three percent of the rice harvest. While this tax rate was very light, the actual weight of the rice taken in through the *so* tax was heavy indeed. Consequently, as a rule the rice itself remained in the *kuni* where it had been grown, and was used to meet local government expenses.

Two other taxes—*chō* and *yō*—were referred to together as corvée labor taxes (*kayaku*) and were levied only on able-bodied men in their prime. The *chō* was a tax levied in kind and in services. It was imposed on local products other than rice, and the expense and physical effort of delivering the payment in kind was also part of the tax. The *yō* tax was also originally a labor tax—ten days' service was required—but products were later substituted for labor. As the goods received as the *chō* and *yō* taxes were light in weight, they were forwarded to the capital and used to finance the expenses of the central government. Households (*ko*) that bore these two taxes also bore the responsibility for transporting the tax-in-kind payments to the capital. Inasmuch as these head taxes were imposed indiscriminately on all people regardless of their wealth, they constituted an extremely heavy burden for the poor. Moreover, the *kuni* administration could extract up to sixty days of corvée labor from *chō* and *yō* taxpayers. This surtax, called the *zōyō* ("miscellaneous tax"), was often appropriated by *kokushi* for their own private purposes, and became one cause of great suffering. The heavy burden of these taxes sometimes led people to desert their permanent homes and become vagrants.

6. The Judicial System and Penal Law

a) The Judicial System. The *ritsuryō* system divided judicial proceedings into two types, *soshō* (civil litigation) and *dangoku* (criminal suits). Trials of civil suits were held during the five months between harvest (October) and planting (February), and complaints could be filed only during this period. Criminal suits as a rule were instituted by indictments from the *danjōdai* and by complaints from injured parties and the general public. In principle, confessions were required in order for guilty verdicts to be returned. Hence, when the accused refused to acknowledge his crime, despite strong presumption of guilt, he was often tortured to elicit a confession. Verdicts of guilt had to cite the exact passages of the *ritsuryō kyakushiki* which formed the basis of judgment. This practice was adopted not to protect the criminal's rights but to demonstrate the necessity for strict adherence to the sovereign's legal commands in important matters like the punishment of criminals.

b) Penal Law. Penalities and punishments sanctioned by the *ritsuryō* codes were enumerated in the *ritsu*. The main point of *ritsu* was to chastise and rehabilitate criminals so that they would not again commit crimes. Punishments were also intended to deter the general populace from misbehavior. Conduct deemed evil by Confucian standards was regarded with great severity. The *ritsu* provided for five kinds of punishment: flogging, beating, forced labor, exile, and death. Operating on the moral premise that it was as wrong to be impenitent as it was to commit a misdemeanor, judicial officers usually remitted punishment if the transgressor contritely surrendered before his crime had been discovered.

C. Government by Imperial Advisors
First Half of the Heian Era, 810–967

1. Decline of the Daijōkan

In the Nara era, Japan was governed under despotic imperial rule through the Chinese-style *daijōkan*. However, this form of government disintegrated during the Heian era. The Heian era began in 794, when Emperor Kanmu founded a new capital in Kyoto and continued until 1185, the time of the establishment of the Kamakura *bakufu*. The *daijōkan* governmental system was originally based on the system of land allotment and household registration. During the Heian era these institutions gradually disappeared, and the *daijōkan* system also gave way to a new administrative form called *sekkan* government. The transition took some time, however, and in the interim there emerged a form of government that entailed management by the emperor's closest advisors (*sokkinsha*). This form was consistent with *ritsuryō* government in that it maintained direct imperial rule (*tennō shinsei*), but the moving force in politics shifted from offices like the *daijōkan* with legal roots in the *ritsuryō* codes to the imperial advisors. The operation of this transitional form of government was typified by offices like the *kurōdo-dokoro* and the *kebiishi*. The *kurōdo-dokoro* was originally an office which procured and stored articles for the emperor's daily use. However, in 810, Emperor Saga began using it as his own private secretariat to handle secret matters. While Saga's objective was simply to circumvent and curb the influence of the retired emperor Heizei, this innocuous office eventually grew to wield enormous powers. The *kebiishi*, too, was originally only a constabulary for arresting criminals in the capital, but in later years its powers expanded to embrace policing, trials, and punishment.

2. Growth of Large-scale Land Ownership

While the land redistribution system continued to operate on a six-year cycle until the end of the Nara era, it faltered because the supply of land required for its proper implementation was inadequate. Moreover, the household registers on which land reapportionment was based gradually became spurious. By the latter half of the tenth century, land redistribution had ceased. As the old land and registration systems crumbled, large-scale private ownership of land increased. As early as 723, the government began permitting those who, providing new irrigation facilities, reclaimed new lands to hold them privately for three generations beyond their own lives, and for their own lifetimes if they used preexisting irrigation works. This program was devised in order to provide incentives for increasing the amount of land which could eventually be redistributed as *kubunden,* but the incentives proved insufficient. Then, in 743, the government agreed that newly opened lands should be private property, immune from confiscation in perpetuity. One may thus conclude that the key to the concept of private ownership rights in Japan was the acknowledgment of perpetual inheritance. Be that as it may, the fact is that this law did spur reclamation work, particularly by influential families, temples, and shrines. Since poor farmers suffered as a result, the government subsequently attempted to terminate all reclamation work. This proved impossible to enforce, however, and in time the evils of large-scale private agglomerations of land reappeared.

CHAPTER 3

THE GROWTH OF *SHŌEN*, THE *BAKUFU*, AND *SHŌEN* FEUDALISM

Chūsei, or Middle Ages, 967–1467

As the *ritsuryō* system declined during the Middle Ages, the law of the archaic period again revived. Of course, remolded in the context of changing social and political conditions, this law had acquired many new aspects, so it was not completely restored to its original form.

The early Middle Ages included the latter part of the Heian era, from 967 to 1185. The evolving rights of ownership of large estates immune to imperial interference were now combined with rights in public law in a development leading to a new landed institution, the *shōen*. A new class, the *bushi* (warriors), also emerged at this time. Politically these two developments were closely related. In 1185, the court appointed Minamoto-no-Yoritomo as *sō-shugo* (chief of military governors) and *sō-jitō* (chief of military land stewards), and he in turn appointed his retainers (*gokenin*) to be either *shugo* (military governors) of the *kuni* or *jitō* (stewards) in *shōen* and *kōryō* (public lands), thus linking the *bushi* organization to the *shōen* politically. Through his *jitō* rights (*jitō-shiki*), Yoritomo acquired control over the possession of a portion of the *shōen* and *kōryō* lands, *i.e.*, the right to grant income from these lands to his vassals, and on this basis he established his *bakufu* (literally, "tent [or warrior] government"). The creation of the *bakufu* marked the inception of feudalism as well as the end of the early Middle Ages. Since the Kamakura *bakufu* was founded by invading the *shōen*, feudalism in this era can be called *shōen*-style feudalism.

In the ensuing Kamakura era (1185–1333), equilibrium was more or less maintained between the *shōen* and the feudal organization, but at the beginning of the Muromachi era (1333–1467) civil war upset the balance and *bushi* invaded the *shōen* at an increasing pace. The Muromachi *bakufu* was built, like its Kamakura predecessor, on the balance between *shōen* and feudal power; and as civil war between the northern and southern courts* raged throughout the country, the *bakufu*'s stability was steadily undermined. In short, the *shōen* and *shōen*-style feudalism declined during the Muromachi era, and as the *bakufu*'s authority weakened, the *shugo* in the countryside increasingly came to resemble local feudal lords. This trend culminated in a prolonged series of civil wars in the beginning of the early modern period (the *sengoku* era), bringing the Middle Ages to an end with the Muromachi era.

It should be added that the old court nobility (*kuge*) still enjoyed considerable power at the outset of the Middle Ages. Indeed, Yoritomo was able to establish *shugo* and *jitō* posts by court sanction alone. Later, however, especially after the Jōkyū War,** the *bakufu* was able to reduce the influence of the imperial court, and by the time of the Muromachi era the court had become virtually powerless. In this sense, the Middle Ages were a time of transition between the ancient period, when the emperor enjoyed full political power, and the early modern period (*kinsei*), in which all vestiges of imperial power disappeared.

A. The *Kuge* Political System
Second Half of the Heian Era, 967–1185

By the last half of the Heian era, court officials were known as *kuge* (nobles). The court-centered order of this era is therefore called the *kuge* political system.

1. Sekkan System

A *sesshō* (regent) was appointed when the reigning emperor had not yet reached majority; the regent served as his representative

---

* From 1336 to 1392, there were two imperial courts, the "northern court" in Kyoto supported by the Muromachi *bakufu* and the opposing "southern court" in Yoshino, south of Kyoto.

** The "Jōkyū War" occurred when Retired Emperor Go-toba attempted to overthrow the *bakufu* by military force, and was defeated.

in all official matters. A *kanpaku* (chief imperial advisor) was selected to assume control over the administrative apparatus even when the emperor had reached majority. Appointments to both of these posts were made as early as the latter part of the ancient period, but only in unusual circumstances. After 967, however, appointments to these positions were made on a regular basis, creating the *sekkan* (*sesshō-kanpaku*) system and inaugurating the period in Japanese history known as the Middle Ages. The system continued to exist formally until the Meiji Restoration in 1868, but appointees to these two posts controlled politics only until 1185, when their influence was displaced by the political primacy of retired emperors in what is called the *insei* system.

At this time these posts were filled exclusively by members of the Fujiwara family, particularly by the descendants of Fujiwara no Yoshifusa, the first non-imperial prince to hold the post of *sesshō*. Whether the emperor was a minor, occasioning the appointment of a *sesshō*, or had reached his majority, in which case a *kanpaku* was installed, he surrendered all political control to the appointee. While the legal positions of *sesshō* and *kanpaku* differed, the holder of either post dominated politics, reviving the tradition of imperial divorce from political affairs. The use of *sekkan* government in the wake of the collapse of the *ritsuryō* system may be seen as a revival of the archaic institution of rule by *ōomi* and *ōmuraji*. It is important to note that most political decisions in this system were made in the Fujiwara family chancery, called the *mandokoro*. While in fact the holder of the *sesshō* or *kanpaku* post was usually the father of the reigning emperor's mother, that relationship was a personal rather than an officially institutionalized one. Thus, the practice of deciding public affairs of state in private family councils epitomized one of the central characteristics of the Middle Ages—the confluence of personal or individual power and civil, officially recognized authority.

2. Insei System

The term *insei* refers to the type of political control that succeeded the *sekkan* system. It means, quite simply, that political control gradually came into the hands of emperors who had already retired. This exercise of power began when the Fujiwara had begun to decline, and an emperor unrelated to the Fujiwara house became sovereign. In 1068 the new emperor, Go-sanjō, laid plans to revive the *ritsuryō* political system in place of the political control and style of the *sekkan*. Go-sanjō reduced the position of the *kanpaku* (then Fujiwara no Norimichi) to a meaningless post and proceeded to carry out what amounted to a restoration of direct imperial rule. The retired emperor also sought to perpetuate this arrangement, and to prevent the resuscitation of *sekkan* influence he abdicated in favor of his chosen successor, Shirakawa, and for a while was able to counteract Fujiwara influence and maintain control over succession to the throne.

Go-sanjō's *insei* was designed to preserve the emperor's right to exercise imperial authority; it thus differed somewhat from the policies of the next emperor, Shirakawa, whose purpose was simply to enhance the office of retired emperor. From Go-sanjō's death in 1073 to 1086, Shirakawa exercised direct control over the government as emperor. He then violated his late father's wishes by retiring in favor of his seven-year-old son, who became Emperor Horikawa. Although Shirakawa retired, he did not transfer his political power to the new child-emperor but continued to rule as retired emperor. Two later Heian-era emperors, Toba and Go-shirakawa, followed Shirakawa's example over the course of a century, which has since become known as the era of *insei* rule.

Insei rule resembled its predecessor, the *sekkan* system, in many respects. The office (*in*) of the retired emperor was outside the court and served as the locus for deciding important matters of state, while the court was left with little more to do than invest courtiers with their ranks and officiate at ceremonies and other special events. Just as *sekkan* rule was carried out by the maternal grandfather of the emperor, political power under the *insei* system was controlled by the emperor's father or grandfather. Hence, in both the *sekkan* and *insei* systems, personal or individual relationships proved the main determinants of civil affairs, resulting in a blurring of the lines between personal and public concerns.

3. Kuge-Buke Political Order

During the retirement of Emperor Go-shirakawa, the *insei* style of political rule gave way to joint political hegemony by the court nobility (*kuge*) and warrior houses (*buke*). Under the leader-

ship of the Taira (or Heike) family* headquartered in the Rokuhara district of Kyoto, Taira no Kiyomori, of *bushi* origins, rose
from one high court position to another, finally becoming *daijō
daijin*, while his kinsmen monopolized other key posts. The Heike
exercised control by virtue of their enormous financial and military power as well as through their official positions at court; but
they could not have come to power without allying themselves
with the retired emperor Go-shirakawa. Hence, Taira hegemony
was built on a fusion of the *insei* with Heike strength, and may be
considered a continuation of the *insei* style of political rule. On the
other hand, Heike dominance was a forerunner of the political
eminence enjoyed by the warrior class under the Kamakura *bakufu* system. It may therefore be most accurately described as a
transitional stage of political development between the *insei* system
and the rule of the warrior houses.

4. Growth of the Shōen

During the Nara era, large-scale landowners adopted the T'ang
practice of setting aside parcels of land (*chuang*) by building housing and storage facilities for managing them. In Japan, these parcels of land were called *shō*, a term which subsequently took on the
meaning of "newly cultivated fields" (*konden*). In China and in
Nara Japan, the *shō* served only as an economic institution, but
by the Middle Ages in Japan the *shōen* institution had become
legally exempt from taxation or entry by officials of the imperial
court. Tax-exempt *shōen* made their initial appearance late in the
early period, but in the Middle Ages they were commonplace.
The special exemption from official entry was originally obtained
to prevent tax collectors of the *kokushi* from entering the land to
collect revenues. As *shōen* became commonplace, however, this
exemption was widely applied to all spheres of official jurisdiction,
and the master (*ryōshu*) of the *shōen* acquired full authority—
administrative and judicial—within his territory.

Privately held *shōen* thus acquired public powers and became a
symbol of the confluence of individual and civil authority. Landowners obtained exemptions through applications to the government, which then issued certificates declaring the lands to be new

* "Taira" was the *uji* name; "Heike" means "the house of Taira."

shōen. Shōen established through this procedure were legally sanctioned, but many other landowners simply declared their lands *shōen* without going through the proper procedures. While government officials issued frequent prohibitions against this abuse, only the edict of Emperor Go-sanjō in 1069 had any effect. In the long run, the government proved unable to eradicate the practice.

The owners of *shōen* were generally called *ryōshu* (or *ryōke* if they had a third-degree court rank or higher), but in their exercise of public powers they were designated *honjo.* A *ryōshu* set part of the *shōen* aside specifically for himself, and had peasants or corvée laborers in the *shōen* till it. He assigned the rest of his lands to others in return for a portion of their crop *(nengu)* and a service duty *(kuji).* Service duties were of two kinds: *zōji* and *zōyaku.* The *zōji* tax was a newer version of the *chō (mitsugi)* levy on local products and their transport to the tax recipient. The *zōyaku* was the newer version of the old *yō* tax, and specified a fixed number of days each year to be devoted to labor for the *ryōshu.* Those who tilled land in the *shōen* were called *shōmin;* they obtained the right to work the land through application to the *ryōshu.*

The *ryōshu* used a number of officials, called *shōkan,* to manage the land and control the *shōmin.* The most important of these officials were the *kumon* (accountant or bookkeeper), *tadokoro* (supervisor of fields), and *kebiishi* (police). The general manager and representative of the *ryōshu* in the *shōen* was the *azukari-dokoro.* In compensation for fulfilling the duties of these posts *(shiki),* the *ryōshu* provided his officials with lands within the *shōen* that were exempt from levies in kind and in services *(kyūden)* or simply exempt from the *zōji* tax *(kyūmyō).* Some official posts in the central government had become hereditary in this era and were transformed into the right to receive income. The same tendency was reflected in the *shōen,* where the posts *(shiki)* became synonomous with *kyūden* and *kyūmyō.* The *shiki* became regarded as usufructs, and in time the word was applied not only to the *kyūden* and *kyūmyō* lands set aside for compensating *shōen* officials but to all land. In short, the term *shiki* came to connote property rights to real estate.

Honke and *myōshu* were also affiliated with the *shōen* in many cases. The *honke* was an illustrious family of influence, which assumed the responsibility for protecting the *shōen* in return for a specified share of the annual crop and service dues of the *shōen*. The *myōshu* was a legally sanctioned proprietor of *myōden* (*i.e.*, newly developed lands held outside of the *ritsuryō* system); by the end of the Heian era, *shōen* were ordinarily agglomerations of these lands.

5. Emergence of the Bushi

During the latter part of the ancient period, important regional families extended their influence through military strength. They later intermarried with nobles who had come to the countryside after failing ·to gain prominent posts in the central government. In the Middle Ages, this fusion of local military power with the new rural nobility yielded a class of warriors, called *bushi*, who capitalized on the decline of the central government and confusion in local administration to enlarge their power.

The *bushi* established a new type of relationship among themselves, comprising three basic components: *shujin, ie-no-ko,* and *rōtō*. The *ie-no-ko*, "children of the house," were warriors regarded as the "family" (*ichizoku*) of their leaders (the *shujin*). The *rōtō* were less closely related to the leader; they were simply his followers. They pledged to serve the leader loyally, particularly in military affairs; he, in turn, allotted lands or rights to the proceeds of certain lands (*onkyū*) to the *rōtō*. This relationship between leader and retainer was formalized by a certificate (*myōbu*) given to the leader with the retainer's name on it. The combination of leader-retainer ties and *onkyū* ties to the land formed the nexus of private relationships among *bushi*.

During the same period blood-lineage ties among influential rural families were strengthened, and the groups thus formed became competitors for land and power. These groups were identified by a variety of terms, including *ichizoku, ikke, ichimon, ittō, ichiryū*, and *kamon*, but all actually referred to a military alliance between the main line of a family (*honke*) and its branches. The leader (head of the main line of the family) issued military orders to his followers and the heads of the branches of the family. The relationship between family heads and their branch family heads differed in form from the archaic period ties between *uji* chieftain and *uji* members, but it nevertheless represented a resuscitation of the fusion of families with the same name who had belonged to the same clan before its dissolution. In this sense, this relationship had some archaic characteristics. The leader of the blood-lineage group was its military commander, and the leaders of the branch families became his lieutenants. Each of them, in turn, was a *shujin*, who led his own *ie-no-ko* and *rōtō*. Familial groups of warriors organized in this way existed throughout Japan in this period, and by the end of it most of them had aligned themselves with either the Minamoto (Genji) house or the Taira (Heike).

B. *Shōen*-style Feudalism
Kamakura *Bakufu*: Kamakura Era, 1185–1333

1. Chief of the Warrior Houses

In 1185 Minamoto no Yoritomo succeeded in crushing the forces of the Taira, and *bushi* groups throughout the country pledged loyalty to him. The leader of the Minamoto house thus became the leader of all the warrior houses and was thereafter referred to as "*buke no tōryō*" (chief of the warrior houses). This was at first merely a private relationship between Yoritomo and the *bushi*, but it received official recognition later in 1185 when the court granted Yoritomo's request to be entrusted with the rights (*shiki*) of defending the sixty-six provinces (*kuni*) of Japan as *sō-shugo* and *sō-jitō*. His base for carrying out these duties was located in Kamakura, and his administrative functions were called collectively the *bakufu*. As *sō-shugo*, Yoritomo obtained the right to police the entire country. As *sō-jitō*, Yoritomo seized the right to control and dispose of some of the lands held as subtenures on *shōen* and imperial domains (*kōryō*). He appointed vassals directly under him (*gokenin*) to *shugo* posts in each province and to *jitō* positions in *shōen* and imperial domains. He also gained the right to levy a tax of five *shō* (7.5–8 dry quarts) of rice per *tan* for military provisions. It is believed that the proceeds of this tax went in fact to the *jitō*.

The chief of the warriors had three kinds of authority as head of the *bakufu*. First, he was empowered to defend the country (*shugo-ken*) in his capacity as holder of the *sō-shugo shiki*. This was an imperially sanctioned, or official, prerogative, supplemented by the *sō-jito shiki*. Secondly, the *bakufu* enjoyed powers over certain *shōen* as *honjo*. All lands during the Kamakura era were classified as *kuge*-controlled land, lands controlled by *shōen* owners (*honjo*), or warrior lands controlled by the *bakufu*. In the last category, the *bakufu* held the status of *honjo* or *honke*. Inasmuch as the *shōen* represented a confluence of personal and official power, the *bakufu* authority as *honjo* also encompassed both private and official aspects. Finally, the leader of the *bakufu* held the status of supreme leader (*shujin*) in the hierarchy of leader-retainer *bushi* relationships, and therefore had the authority to command the *bushi* in all military affairs.

In short, the powers of the "chief of the warrior houses" were at once official and private. They were supplemented in 1192 when the court bestowed the ancient title of *sei-i-tai-shōgun* (barbarian-subduing generalissimo) on Yoritomo. Some historians argue that this appointment marked the inception of the Kamakura *bakufu*, but judging from Yoritomo's resignation from the post two years later, its significance could not have been that great. We should note, however, that Yoritomo's successors followed his example in obtaining appointment as *shōgun*, and the post later came to symbolize the position of chief of the warriors. Yoritomo's own blood line ended quickly, as his sons Yoriie and Sanetomo died early at the hands of assassins. The next two holders of the *shōgun* post were scions of the Fujiwara house; they, in turn, were followed by four imperial princes. While each of these *shōgun* was formally chief of the warriors, actual authority over the *bushi* was held hereditarily by regents from the Hōjō family. Minamoto no Yoritomo's wife was a member of the Hōjō family, and so this family was able to exercise great power within the *bakufu*.

Even after the *bakufu* was established, the imperial court retained judicial authority over civil litigation between *honjo* and also preserved its authority to appoint and dismiss the *shōgun*. The *kuge* and *bakufu* political orders thus existed side by side. The *bakufu* regarded its regime as existing under the mantle of the imperial throne, so that the emperor continued to rule Japan formally; but under imperial auspices the *bakufu* gained final authority in many areas. For example, although disputes between *honjo* (as *ryōshu* of *shōen*) and *jitō* were at first adjudicated by the imperial court, jurisdiction was later assumed by the *bakufu*.

2. Shōen-style Feudalism

As Yoritomo's position became institutionalized, the leader-retainer relationship, while it retained its personal nature to some extent, also took on a more official character. The "public" and "private" elements were fused in Yoritomo's political position. We refer to the military-political order based on the officially sanctioned *onkyū* and leader-retainer relationships of the *bushi* as "feudalism," or as the *bakufu* political order. Its highest leader was the chief of the warrior houses; the emperor remained outside the framework of these two key relationships.

While the leader-retainer relationship peculiar to the warrior caste was the outgrowth of a spontaneous development among *bushi* toward the end of the Heian era, the *onkyū* system itself was a direct utilization of the preexisting system for assigning posts and lands within the *shōen*. When Yoritomo built his government, he was obliged to look to the *shōen* of influential families for the financial resources to provide *onkyū* for his vassals. Initially, he drew upon confiscated Heike lands bestowed on him by the court. Later, he sought the authority to compensate his vassals by offering them *jitō-shiki* and other rights to the profits of *shōen* lands. In short, rather than abolishing the *shōen*, Yoritomo built a feudal system on them. Japanese feudalism in the Middle Ages was therefore based on a combination of the familial-style leader-retainer relationships among warriors with the *shōen*-style *onkyū* system established under the legal system of the *honjo* to remunerate officials. It may thus be clearly distinguished from the feudalism of the early modern period (*kinsei*), which was erected on an impersonal leader-retainer system (*tōshuteki shūjū-sei*) and a village communal system sanctioned by *bushi* law.

a) The Familial Leader-Retainer System. As we noted earlier, the Middle Ages saw the evolution of a vertical relationship among warriors with Yoritomo and his successors presiding over their vassals (*gokenin*), the leaders of the warrior houses, followed by the leaders of the branch families, and finally by the *ie-no-ko* and *rōtō*. When the *bakufu* wished to mobilize its vassals, the order was passed first to the main house leaders, who communicated it to their branch house leaders and led their retainers into service. The highest duty of the direct vassals was to march into battle with their *rōtō* in response to their master's summons. While this leader-follower relationship has been called "warrior-like," we have noted that its familial nature strongly resembled the clan-grouping *shizoku* system of the archaic period.

The direct vassals (*gokenin*) of the *bakufu* and their followers (*rōtō*) were bound together in a leader-retainer relationship formalized by the retainer's personal pledge of loyalty (*gezan no shiki*). Once this oath had been taken, the retainer was obliged to give unqualified obedience to his leader and was not permitted to question his orders. The absolute quality of this obedience made this relationship quite different from the vassalage of Western European feudalism, which permitted retainers to appeal to the king.

b) The Shōen-style Onkyū System. In return for their retainers' service and obedience, leaders gave protection and a variety of benefits. These took the form of "favors" (*go-on*) granted by the leader; he was under no formal obligation to compensate his followers. There were three types of "favor" bestowed on *gokenin* by the *bakufu* as their master: confirmation of their domains, grants (*onkyū*) of land rights, and recommendations for court offices and ranks.

The first of these "favors" was in fact a confirmation (*ando*) by the *bakufu* of the retainer's right to hold lands which had previously been his anyway (*honryō*). Through this confirmation, the retainer's domain came under the *bakufu* feudal system. Through the dispensation of *onkyū* land rights, retainers also received new income from the *bakufu*. Retainers usually sought new lands in return for services performed, but the leader was free to reject these requests if he wished to. Land rights received were thus granted "by the favor" (*onkyū*) of the master, and were called *onryō*. It was characteristic of the Kamakura era that grants were originally made not of *shōen* land itself but of various rights (*shiki*) to its yield. Unlike private domains obtained through other means, the rights to *onryō* carried with them various restrictions regarding their disposition. Whether land was *onryō* or private domain confirmed by the *bakufu*, its holder was subject to regular and extraordinary *bakufu* levies, called *kantō mikūji* or *gokeninyaku*. The most important of these taxes on the services of the *gokenin* was *ōban'yaku*, which obliged retainers to spend a part of every year in Kyoto guarding the imperial palace.

The third way in which retainers were compensated by the *bakufu* took the form of nominations for court offices and ranks. Since *gokenin* were not permitted to apply to the court directly for these honors, any court recognition they received was the result of recommendation by the *bakufu*. The receipt of court ranks and posts thus constituted another type of *bakufu* "favor" bestowed on its retainers.

In a sense, the imperially sanctioned *shōen* system may be considered a revival of the *tadokoro* of the archaic period, molded by *ritsuryō* influences. It retained characteristics of the aristocratic society of the ancient period. Feudalism in the Middle Ages was thus comprised of elements developed in earlier periods, notably the familial-style leader-retainer ties and the *shōen*-style *onkyū* system. We shall see, however, that after the close of the Middle Ages, these older elements were no longer an integral part of feudalism. The Middle Ages, then, constituted a transitional stage between the earlier periods of Japanese history and the early modern period (*kinsei*).

Japanese feudalism in the Middle Ages has often been compared with the feudalism of medieval Western Europe. Feudalism in Europe also evolved from the fusion of a retainer system (*Vassallität*) and an *onkyū* system (*Benefizialwesen*), but in two important respects it was quite different from the Japanese case. First, the European system was capped by a monarch, whereas the highest feudal leader in Japan was the chief of the warriors. The Japanese emperor remained outside the nexus of feudal relationships. Second, the leader-retainer relationship in Japan was characterized by obligations incumbent only on the follower, who had to be absolutely obedient to his leader's commands. In Europe, the feudal system was based on reciprocal fidelity between leaders and retainers.

In the latter part of the Heian era it became customary for landholders to divide their domains among their sons prior to their deaths. Through this process, a domain might eventually become so reduced by repeated divisions among heirs as to severely impair the power and prestige of the family. To prevent this unfortunate outcome, it had long been the practice for landholders to have one son take general responsibility and supervise as *sōryō*. To all exterior appearances, the *sōryō* held the rights to all his father's lands, even though the land was formally divided among all the sons.

It became necessary to institutionalize this practice under the Kamakura *bakufu* in order to assure payment of the *kantō mikūji* levies. The *sōryō* now became responsible in his own right for paying the *kūji* of his brothers and other collaterals (*shoshi*) as well as his own. However, this relationship among brothers existed only for the purpose of dealing with pressures outside the family; within the family, there were no formal restrictions placed on the continued subdivision of domains among sons. It was thus only at the end of the Kamakura era that fathers began bequeathing their property to one son alone, enjoining him to leave the property to only one of his sons as well. This custom became the origin of the inheritance law of primogeniture.

3. Changes in the Shōen Institution

The special exemptions from imperial taxation and entry enjoyed by *shōen* holders continued in force during the Kamakura era. However, these exemptions were soon broken down to a considerable degree by the new holders of power, the warrior houses. As we will soon see, the prohibition of entry by government officials was violated by the creation of *shugo* posts throughout the country. To prevent *shugo* officials from entering *shōen* lands, *shōen* holders were obliged to seek additional exemption privileges from the *bakufu* itself.

It was even more difficult to prevent *bushi* violations of *shōen* immunity through the *jitō* institution. The *bakufu* established two types of *jitō*, the *honpo jitō* and *shinpo jitō*. When Yoritomo received the post of *sō-jitō* in 1185, he appointed his retainers to serve as *jitō* in *shōen* and imperial domains, with authority to take five *shō* of rice per *tan*. These *jitō* were called *honpo jitō* ("original appointees"), and they seem to have obtained controlling rights (*chigyō-ken*) over a portion of the *shōen* in which they were placed. By stationing *jitō* in *shōen* and imperial domains, the *bakufu* extended the authority of the warrior houses throughout the country and at the same time obtained sources of income for its *gokenin*. The right to station *jitō* in the *shōen* belonged to the *bakufu*, not to the proprietors of the *shōen*. Although the *kokushi* and the *honjo* were able in 1186 to pressure the *bakufu* into recalling some of the *jitō*, the first step in the destruction of the *shōen* system by the forces of feudalism had been taken.

At the beginning of the thirteenth century, the retired emperor Go-toba laid plans to overthrow the *bakufu* and reassert the authority of the throne in politics. This plan led to the Jōkyū War, which ended in 1221. The victorious *bakufu* confiscated the *shōen* of the *kuge*, temples, and shrines aligned with the ex-emperor. The *jitō* placed in these newly won lands were called *shinpo jitō* ("new appointees"). In recognizing these appointments, the court granted the *jitō* one *chō* (ten *tan*) of tax-exempt land for every additional ten *chō* under their supervision and confirmed their right to the proceeds of a five-*shō*-per-*tan* rice levy for military provisions. These proceeds were formally designated the *shinpo rippō* ("newly instituted ratio").

The creation of the *jitō* post was in itself a heavy blow to the autonomy and special privileges of the *shōen*, but it paled in comparison with the impact of the *jitō*'s abuse of his position. Not only did *jitō* begin appropriating *shōen* tax revenues and services (*nengu*, *kuji*) for themselves, but in time they began to infringe on those parts of the *shōen* to which they did not legally enjoy access. A number of measures were instituted to prevent these abuses. The *jitō* might be made responsible under a formal contract (*jitō uke-dokoro*) for satisfactory collection of all tax revenues and services stipulated as the proprietor's due. If the proprietor of the *shōen* requested, the *bakufu* could formally divide the *shōen* lands in two, granting half to the *jitō* in return for assurances that the other half would remain free from his interference (*shitaji chūbun*). Finally, disputed lands were sometimes divided between proprietor and *jitō* through judicial settlements authorized by *bakufu* courts.* All of these procedures resulted in alienating the proprietor from at least part of his *shōen*, or in reducing the size of his holdings. Nevertheless, throughout the Kamakura era, the *shōen* institution persisted in form and in content, preserving an equilibrium with the forces of feudalism.

4. Bakufu Structure and Local Administration

a) *Bakufu Structure.* Yoritomo presided over a *bakufu* organiza-

---

* Initially, authority to adjudicate cases involving *jitō* infringements on *honjo* lands rested with the imperial court. Shortly after the Jōkyū War, however, Hōjō Yasutoki became regent and decided that the *bakufu* should have jurisdiction over this type of case. The establishment of *bakufu* authority in this area represented the final stage in the creation of the *jitō-shiki* system and, indeed, of the *bakufu* system itself.

tion with three central offices: the *samurai-dokoro* (responsible for controlling the *gokenin*); the *mandokoro* (responsible for financial, legislative, and judicial affairs as well as the affairs of Yoritomo's house); and the *monchūjo* (responsible for minor civil justice). Each of these offices had its origins in organs established by the Heian nobility for management of their house affairs; Yoritomo simply adopted them intact for administering the *bakufu*. After Yoritomo's death, the Hōjō family established hereditary control over the headships (*bettō*) of the *samurai-dokoro* and *mandokoro*, thereby seizing *de facto* control of the *bakufu*. As regents (*shikken*), they exercised power as guardians of the *shōgun* and subsequently established the post of "cosignatory" (*rensho*) to assist the *shikken*. Despite their monopoly of important posts, however, the Hōjō were prudent civil administrators who avoided any manifestation of despotic rule. They established a Council of Advisers (*hyōjō-shū*) through which other influential families might deliberate important matters; they also later established a judicial council of hearing officers (*hikitsuke*) through which other familes could share in the adjudication of suits.

b) Local Administration. While the court continued to rely on locally resident officials to manage the imperial domains, the *bakufu* established its own local institutions. The most important of these was the post of *shugo*. The *shugo* was responsible in peacetime for conveying *bakufu* orders to the *gokenin* in his area and for ensuring that they carried out their annual guard duties at the imperial palace. In times of war, he was charged with the responsibility of leading the *gokenin* into battle. He had important police duties as well, and could pursue rebels, murderers, and perpetrators of other severe crimes into imperial or *shōen* domains. If, however, the *bakufu* had granted immunity from *shugo* entry to the *shōen*, the *shugo* could only proceed to the border of the *shōen* and receive custody of fugitives from *shōen* authorities. Nevertheless, by placing *shugo* in each province, the *bakufu* established a nationwide network for controlling the *gokenin* and established its prerogative to try all perpetrators of severe crimes. Combined with the widespread creation of *jitō* posts, the appointment of *shugo* permitted *bakufu* influence to permeate the entire country. In time, Hōjō family members acquired a monopoly on appointments to *shugo* positions.

After the Jōkyū War, the *bakufu* established the office of "deputy" (*tandai*) based in the Rokuhara district of Kyoto. This official was responsible not only for the policing of the capital and western provinces, but also for maintaining a steady watch on the activities of the court. Similarly, in 1296, after the conclusion of the second Mongol invasion, a *tandai* office was permanently established in Kyushu. *Tandai* in both places had judicial authority as well as police and military functions.

5. The *Goseibai Shikimoku* of 1232

From a legal standpoint, the most outstanding characteristic of the Kamakura era was that three systems of law existed side by side. The law applied by the court to the lands and people under *kuge* proprietorship was called *kuge hō*; the law followed by proprietors of *shōen* within their domains was referred to as *honjo hō*; and the law established by the *bakufu* over the lands and people of warrior domains was *buke hō*. Needless to say, *buke hō* was the most important of the three legal systems during this era. Written law promulgated by the regent Hōjō Yasutoki in the fifty-one-article *Goseibai Shikimoku*, often called the *Jōei Shikimoku* because it was issued in the first year of the Jōei era (1232). The *Goseibai Shikimoku* was predicated on the body of customary law prevalent in the Middle Ages and was aimed merely at amending, supplementing, or defining this customary law. Yasutoki himself indicated that he wished to provide a general written statement of these laws to prevent judges from handing down arbitrary or unfair decisions, varying according to the individuals involved or the particular situation under legal challenge. The formulary contained only fifty-one articles, however, and was in this sense very different from the *ritsuryō* codes. Subsequent additions to the code were made in the form of specific ordinances called "addenda" (*tsuika*).

6. The Judicial System and Penal Law

a) *The Judicial System*. At this juncture, the system of *jitō* rights had come fully into its own, and the *bakufu* was at the height of its powers. At first, cases of violation of *honjo* rights by *jitō* were adjudicated by imperial courts, but after the Jōkyū War they fell within the trial jurisdiction of the *bakufu*. In its developed form, the judicial system of the *bakufu* distinguished three types of judicial process.

Shomu-zata was the process used in adjudicating lawsuits related to proprietorship. *Zatsu-zata* was for litigation over movable estates and obligations, and *kendan-zata* was employed in trying criminal cases. Of these, *shomu-zata* was the most sophisticated. The high level of development here was probably a result of the fact that landed property then constituted the bulk of private wealth, and lawsuits contesting property rights were intimately related to the existence of the *bakufu* itself. The Hōjō, who were attentive to civil administration, were especially sensitive to the critical nature of this type of litigation, and thus fostered a high degree of refinement in adjudicating cases involving property claims. Each case was considered in a preliminary hearing by a council of hearing officers expressly established by the Hōjō to consider litigation (*hikitsuke*). After this council drafted a decision, their draft was forwarded to the council of *bakufu* advisors (*hyōjōshū*) to be approved or rejected by majority vote. It is significant that heavy emphasis was laid on producing a just verdict, irrespective of the individuals involved in litigation.

We should also note that when affidavits or testimony were questionable, courts in the Middle Ages resorted to seeking divine guidance on their value, just as in the archaic period. The witness in question was first obliged to submit a written oath affirming the honesty and truthfulness of his testimony. He was then interned in the main building of a Shintō shrine for a fixed number of days. The veracity of his testimony and oath was affirmed by the gods if, during his confinements, none of a series of inauspicious incidents specified by the *bakufu* occurred. If one of these accidents did occur, the witness's testimony was held to be invalid.

b) Penal Law. The *ritsuryō* penal law was conceived as a means of enlightening the people and enabling them to approximate Confucian ideals of behavior. Penal law in the Middle Ages was more pragmatic, aiming primarily at the preservation of the feudal system and feudal morality. Punishments were devised from this pragmatic viewpoint as well. The most common punishment was the confiscation of land, reflecting the great significance of landed property during this period.

B. The Decay of Shōen-Style Feudalism and Centralized Government
Muromachi Era, 1333–1467

1. The Changing Nature of the "Buke no Tōryō"

The Kamakura *bakufu* fell in 1333, and direct imperial rule was temporarily restored under Emperor Go-daigo. However, this "Kenmu Restoration" lasted only three years. Ashikaga Takauji soon became leader of the military houses, and established his *bakufu* in 1338. The third *shōgun* of his line, Ashikaga Yoshimitsu, completed his grandfather's work in organizing the new *bakufu* and placed its headquarters in the Muromachi section of Kyoto.

Under the Muromachi *bakufu*, the position of the *"buke no tōryō"* differed considerably from what it had been during the Kamakura era. Except for Yoritomo, previous *tōryō* had held power in name only, while regents exercised actual political control. In the Muromachi era power was usually exercised directly by the *shōgun* as chief of the warriors. Moreover, in the Kamakura era the *bakufu*—as the office of the *tōryō*—had existed independently of the court aristocracy; indeed, the *bakufu* and court institutions stood formally in opposition to one another. In contrast, the prerogatives of the *tōryō* during the Muromachi era enabled him to exercise control over the court nobility (*kuge*) as well as the military houses. However, it should be noted that the apparent power of the *tōryō* vis-à-vis the *kuge* and within the *bakufu* was not so strong. The *tōryō* appeared to be more powerful, but the political strength of the *kuge* and the *bakufu* itself was actually declining only in comparison to the Kamakura era.

While there were thus significant differences between the Kamakura and Muromachi *bakufu* systems, there was also considerable continuity between the two eras. The Muromachi *bakufu*, for example, retained the *Goseibai Shikimoku* as its basic law.

2. The Decay of Shōen-Style Feudalism

We have noted that Kamakura feudalism was based on the *on-kyū* system of benefices within the *shōen* and the familial style of leader-retainer relationships among warriors. Both of these systems underwent radical transformation during the Muromachi era, and the nature of feudalism was profoundly affected.

Early in the Muromachi era, the imperial court was rent by civil war and divided openly into two factions. A northern court and sourthern court were established, and warriors throughout Japan aligned themselves with one or the other to legitimize their wanton seizure of lands from *shōen* proprietors (*honjo-ryō*). *Shōen* proprietors were dealt an additional blow by the enactment of the *hanzei* law, which permitted *bakufu* authorities to withhold half of the *shōen* revenues in the name of financing military campaigns. These attacks on the *shōen* system were accompanied by the proliferation of lands within the *shōen* which were not specifically assigned to holders of *shiki*. *Onkyū* within the *shōen* system had taken the form of an award of a *shiki*; accordingly, the increase of lands not held under *shiki* rights meant the decline of *shōen*-type *onkyū*.

The familial style of leader-retainer relationships was also undermined during the Muromachi era. It became a universal practice for family heads to leave their domains to only one heir and to forbid division of the inheritance by future generations. Later the *bakufu* stipulated that lands bestowed on its retainers could be inherited only by the eldest sons. With the development of the practice of primogeniture, the entire family system and the familial style of leader-retainer relationships, both of which had been based on a system of divided inheritance, were severely compromised. In turn, then, the *shōen*-type *onkyū* system, which was based on this familial-style leader-retainer relationship, was weakened and began to collapse.

3. The Growth of Shugo-held Provinces

The struggle between the northern and southern courts had many political, economic, and social ramifications. For example, the continued existence of a rival southern court in Yoshino obliged Ashikaga Takauji to remain in Kyoto to protect the northern court, which supported him. His *bakufu* was therefore established in the imperial capital, not in Kamakura. A second consequence of the civil wars of the fourteenth century was the acceleration of the collapse of the *shōen* system, as we have already seen. A third, and highly significant, result of the protracted struggle among courtiers and warriors was that *bakufu* authority could no longer be effectively exercised at the local level, and control over local political and economic affairs was seized by the *shugo*.

The *shugo* were originally no more than local *bakufu* officials who lacked even the authority to collect taxes. During the Muromachi era, however, they usurped this authority, converted the *jitō* into their personal retainers, and used the provisions of the *hanzei* law arbitrarily to misappropriate lands from *shōen* held by temples, shrines, and other proprietors. They used the proceeds from these tax levies and land seizures to remunerate their growing body of retainers. The more powerful *shugo* not only ignored *bakufu* orders, but issued legal proclamations as if they came from the *shōgun* and proceeded to hold trials when they were violated. In general, the *shugo* behaved as if the areas under their jurisdiction were their own domains; and indeed, the term used to describe a *shugo* territory, *bunkoku* ("appropriated province"), implied as much.

4. Structure of the Muromachi Bakufu and Local Administration

The Muromachi equivalent of the post of regent (*shikken*) was *shitsuji* and, later, *kanrei*. Since the *shōgun* directly supervised *bakufu* affairs, however, the *kanrei* was merely an auxiliary official, in contrast to the powerful regents of the Kamakura era. The office of the *mandokoro* handled the *shōgun*'s financial and house affairs, as well as minor civil litigation. The *monchūjo* had responsibility for keeping and certifying official documents and dealing with lawsuits involving forgery. The *samurai-dokoro* was in charge of policing the noble and warrior houses and exercised criminal jurisdiction within the city of Kyoto.

Although his *bakufu* was located in Kyoto, Takauji recognized the great political importance of the Kantō district and dispatched close relatives to Kamakura as *kanrei* to govern the district. In time, the *kanrei* became a hereditary post, and eventually it became independent of the *bakufu*. Its holder began calling himself *kubō* (a title formerly reserved for the *shōgun*), and the title of *kanrei* was given to his assistant.

The sources of income of the Muromachi *bakufu* differed from those of the Kamakura *bakufu*. Once the *bakufu* had been established in the imperial capital, it obtained an important part of its financial resources by levying taxes on the commercial enterprises of Kyoto, particularly *saké* brewers and pawn shops.

5. Judicial System and Penal Law

Earlier, we indicated that the Kamakura judicial system recognized three types of proceedings: *shomu-zata*, *zatsumu-zata*, and *kendan-zata*. The Muromachi *bakufu* followed this precedent, and set up separate courts to deal with each procedure. In time, the procedures became identified in terms of the courts in which they took place. Hence, *shomu-zata* became *hikitsuke-zata* (after the *hikitsuke-shū*, or judicial council, established to settle disputes dealing with land matters); *zatsumu-zata* became *mandokoro-zata;* and *kendan-zata* became *samurai-dokoro-zata*. The *hikitsuke-zata* were subsequently called *gozen-zata*. Proceedings related to lawsuits occasioned by errors in documents were called *monchūjo-zata*.

Under the Muromachi *bakufu*, trial by ordeal was often practiced in certain types of cases. The process of divination was called *yugishō* (trial by scalding water) and represented a revival of the *kukadachi* of the archaic period.

We should also take note of two trends in penal law during the Muromachi era. First, the Kamakura *bakufu* had worked to restrict the application of *renza* and *enza*, earlier concepts of criminal liability without fault,* but during the Muromachi era, in response to the lawless spirit of the times, the application of these concepts became more harsh.

Second, laws were developed punishing both parties to a fight. In 1346, the *bakufu* ruled that, in case of an armed conflict, the attacker would always be criminally liable, and the defender also, unless he were in the right at the outset of the dispute. In 1352, it was ruled that both were to be punished in all cases, but with a lesser degree of punishment for a defender in the right. By the end of the fifteenth century, it had become the rule to regard both combatants as joint offenders, equally guilty.

---

* *"Enza"* and *"renza"* were originally *ritsuryō* terms. They differed in that the former indicated criminal liability of the relatives of a major offender; the latter, that of unrelated persons serving in the same official bureau. Article 10 of the *Goseibai Shikimoku* provided that *enza* should not be applied to the father of a murderer, if he was unaware of the crime. By the mid-Kamakura era, *renza* was being applied in some cases to the neighbors of a criminal offender, and its scope was gradually extended during the Muromachi era.

CHAPTER 4

FROM DECENTRALIZED FEUDALISM (*SENGOKU* ERA) TO UNIFIED FEUDALISM (EDO ERA)

Kinsei, or Early Modern Period, 1467–1858

The early modern period may be divided into three separate phases of historical and legal development. The first of these phases extends from 1467 to 1587 and coincides roughly with the *sengoku*, or "warring states," era. The second phase extends from 1587 to 1742 and covers roughly the first half of the Edo era. The final phase includes the 116 years between 1742 and 1858, during the last half of the Edo era.

The *sengoku* era was characterized by the growth of powerful and independent local territorial and military magnates called *daimyō*. In the context of legal history, it may be regarded as a period in which legal authority was fragmented. During this period the *shōen* system continued to erode, and it was finally abolished by Toyotomi Hideyoshi's cadastral survey (*taikō ken-chi*) at the end of the sixteenth century. The village (*mura*) now replaced the *shōen* as the basic unit of the feudal fief, and the familial-style leader-retainer relationship was replaced by a new style focused on the *yori-oya* ("protector"). These developments set the stage for the evolution of a new type of feudalism in the Edo era.

In 1587 Hideyoshi completed the task of unifying the independent *daimyō* of the *sengoku* era when he accepted the surrender of the Shimazu, a house long powerful in Kyushu. This event marked the beginning of the second phase of the early modern period. Hideyoshi's control over the *daimyō* passed to Tokugawa

Ieyasu after the battle of Sekigahara in 1600. Ieyasu recognized that the power of the Toyotomi family had rested solely on the strength of Hideyoshi and that Hideyoshi's death in 1598 weakened the family dangerously. When setting up his own *bakufu* in Edo, therefore, Ieyasu sought to assure its permanence by careful attention to organization and institutions. He took great care when placing *daimyō* in strategic areas and issued a detailed body of directives (*Buke-sho-hatto*) to which *daimyō* were required to conform. Other restrictions regulated the activities of the imperial court and religious institutions.

The second phase of the early modern period thus marked the zenith of feudal development in Japan. During the first half of the Edo era, the most important officials in the *bakufu* were those who dealt with military affairs. However, midway through the eighteenth century, officials concerned with civil administration began to supersede their counterparts in military affairs as the *bakufu*'s most important officials. This shift in priorities reflected the beginning of the decay of feudalism. It was symbolized by the promulgation in 1742 of a *bakufu* legal code called the *Kujikata Osadamegaki* that marked the beginning of the final phase of the early modern period.

During the early modern period all land in Japan became the domain of the warrior houses, and Japanese society itself was "feudalized." Based on vassalage bonds between unrelated household heads and village units incorporated by warrior law, the feudalism of the early modern period was completely shorn of prefeudal elements and contained, as we shall see, the seeds of modernity. This was a phenomenon unique to Japan. No European society ever experienced this type of unified feudalism, and European feudalism even at its zenith was completely antithetical to the concept of modernity.

A. Decentralized Feudalism
Sengoku Era, 1467–1587

1. Decentralized Feudalism

The *sengoku* era began with the outbreak of the Ōnin War in 1467. Confrontations among the *shugo* and lesser local magnates had been frequent, but only after 1467 did Japan actually enter an age in which survival and political power depended solely on military strength. Local provincial lords became independent of *bakufu* control and gradually evolved into the prototypes of the Edo-era *daimyō*. The Muromachi *bakufu* survived, but its authority existed in name alone. Actual political power was divided among the local military magnates; the feudalism of this era was distinctly decentralized. While these local lords were being reunified, first by Oda Nobunaga and then by Toyotomi Hideyoshi, the basis for feudalism in the medieval period—the familial-style leader-retainer relationship and the *shōen*-style *onkyū* system—was changing into a village-*onkyū* system and a "protector" style of leader-retainer relationship during the *sengoku* era.

The vertical relationship binding suzerain and main house leaders—who served as his direct retainers (*kashin*)—to their branch house leaders and, finally, to the *ie-no-ko* and *rōtō* was based in the Middle Ages on a system of inheritance which preserved established economic relations and familial ties among warrior sons by dividing their father's legacy among them. Perpetuation of these relationships permitted the survival of blood-lineage groups unified under main house leaders. However, this familial style of leader-retainer relationship inevitably collapsed after the end of the Kamakura era, when inheritance changed to a system based on primogeniture. As the older ties binding the military unit together were severed, there emerged a new style of warrior relations under the locally based chief. His *kashin* and the large numbers of foot soldiers they recruited (*hikan*) became formally related as *yori-oya* "(protectors" or "quasi-parents") and *yori-ko* ("protected" or "quasi-children"). The *yori-oya* stood as intermediaries between suzerain and *yori-ko* in peacetime, transmitting orders from ruler to *yori-ko* or relaying their requests to him. In wartime the *yori-oya* led the *yori-ko* into battle.

The Kamakura warrior submitted to the chief of the warriors (*buke no tōryō*) only indirectly, through the head of the main branch of his house. By the *sengoku* era, however, the strength of hereditary relations between main and branch house leaders had been fatally compromised by the growth of primogeniture. Therefore, the ruler insisted that all incumbent house leaders, not simply main house leaders, be directly responsible for obedience to his commands. Succeeding rulers insisted on reconfirming this obedience. Rulers and house leaders entered into direct and personal relationships on the basis of these pledges of loyalty and obedience, paving the way for a new leader-retainer relationship in the Edo era.

The collapse of the *shōen* system terminated the practice of *onkyū*, in which various *shiki* to lands within the *shōen* were received as benefices. It therefore became customary to repay services with direct land grants (*chigyōchi*). Taxes came to be no longer levied on those who enjoyed rights in the *shōen*, but on the villages located on the land. Villagers were responsible for paying these taxes. These developments were fostered by the land surveys of Oda Nobunaga and Toyotomi Hideyoshi, which regarded the village as the basic economic unit. As the village became the basic unit of land granted as feudal fiefs, a new *onkyū* system emerged—the village-*onkyū* system. Although there were some instances where rice, rather than land, was bestowed on retainers for their services, the village-*onkyū* system became an integral element of feudalism in the Edo era.

One unique manifestation of the importance of military service in *sengoku* warrior relationships was the appearance of *jindai* and *bandai* (guardians of *kashin* who had not yet reached manhood, usually below their fifteenth year). These guardians were appointed by the suzerain or with his permission. Their primary duty was to execute the military responsibilities of their charges rather than simply to serve the interests of the *kashin*. The *jindai* or *bandai* administered the domain of the young *kashin*, ran his family affairs, executed his feudal services to the ruler, and was further obliged to provide him with financial assistance when necessary.

2. Growth of Villages and Cities

By the end of the *sengoku* era, the *shōen* had almost totally disintegrated, and villages had been formed in their place. Villages as legal entities appeared first in the Kamakura era, and proliferated during the Muromachi. During the *sengoku* era, their internal cohesiveness was strengthened by villagers' common interest in defending the village, maintaining its water-works, and supporting its main shrines. Land proprietors capitalized on members' solidarity to make villagers collectively responsible for payment of taxes, while penal law held the village collectively responsible for transgressions of its members. Political leadership was exercised by those holding positions called *sata-nin* or *otona*, and village rules, known as *sōjū-okite* or *sōshō-okite*, were determined by a conference of villagers, which also punished violators. These institutions and laws were the precursors of the village system of the Edo era.

While there had long been a thriving urban life in seats of political power like Nara, Kyoto, and Kamakura and in port towns and around important temples and shrines, no city was ever centered on a concentration of warrior residences prior to the *sengoku* era. Warriors had built residences on the plains (*hirashiro*) for normal use and mountain strongholds (*yamashiro*) for use during battle. The *sengoku daimyō*, however, began building their castle-homes on strategically located hilltops and had their *kashin* live in the shadow of the castle in nearby areas. Merchants and craftsmen were induced to join this residential complex, and markets were opened under the *daimyō*'s protection. Cities created in this fashion were called *jōkamachi*, and included Odawara under the protection of the Hōjō family, Kōfu under the Takeda, Sunpu (now Shizuoka) under the Imagawa, Kiyosu under the Oda, Yamaguchi under the Ōuchi, and Funai (now Ōita) under the Ōtomo. Cities near harbors and in the precincts of important religious institutions also developed spectacularly. They included Sakai, Kuwano, and Yamada, and some of them acquired considerable autonomy. Sakai, for example, was regarded as an independent city-state.

3. Organization of Provincial Domains (Bunkoku)

The organization of *daimyō* provinces varied according to locale but generally reflected, even in peacetime, a military system of preparedness for warfare. Quasi-familial terminology characterized the institutions and affairs of the domain. Its political affairs, for instance, were referred to as "house affairs" (*kamu*). The chief political administrators were called house elders (*karō*) or, at lower levels, simply elders (*toshiyori, churō*). There were clerks (*yūhitsu*) and investigators (*metsuke, yokome*), as well as financial commissioners (*kanjō bugyō*) and commissioners of temples and shrines (*jisha bugyō*). The government of Oda Nobunaga, the first of Japan's great political unifiers in the sixteenth century, was little more than this type of domain structure writ large, although Nobunaga did establish a special administrative officer (*shoshidai*) in Kyoto to supervise the government of the capital city.

4. Domain Law

Legal authority, like political authority, was decentralized during the *sengoku* era, and each autonomous domain had its own laws. The more important domains tended to codify their legal practices. The best known of these codes are the *Kabegaki* collection of the laws of the Ōuchi family of Suō, the *Kana Mokuroku* of the Imagawa of Suruga, the *Jinkaishū* of the Date of Mutsu, and the first of the two volumes of the *Takeda Shingen Kahō* of the Takeda of Kai. They had a number of features in common. All contained many provisions for the ruler's intervention in determining the status of *kashin*; all contained a wide range of regulations concerning the life of the people; all specified a number of military rules, such as provisos for punishing both parties to a quarrel; and all enunciated a number of "foreign policy" guidelines, particularly with reference to closing their domains off from outside intercourse (*sakoku*). Finally, many of them reflected the influence of the *Goseibai Shikimoku*.

5. The Judicial System and Penal Law

a) The Judicial System. Justice in the various domains often consisted of a continuation of Muromachi judicial practices, but some domains such as that of the Satomi in Awa introduced judicial innovations which served as precursors to the judicial system of the Edo era. Civil proceedings were called *kuji* or *mondō*, while criminal process was called *kendan*. Since the criminal's confession remained a necessary prerequisite for guilty verdicts, torture was often used to prompt the accused to admit to his crime. Methods of torture included sitting the accused astride a wooden horse with heavy stones tied to his ankles (*mokuba*) and shutting him into a water-filled dungeon (*mizurō*).

Many religious institutions had enjoyed the special privilege of asylum since the Kamakura era: this privilege continued to be recognized in some domains while it was abolished in others.

b) Penal Law. In principle, punishment in the *sengoku* era could only be exacted by public institutions; private punishments were not recognized as legitimate. Implication in criminal activity could occur on the basis of blood relationship with the miscreant (*enza*), and sons were often held criminally responsible for their parents' offenses. Implication in the criminal activity of a miscreant through other than familial relationships (*renza*) was also recognized; a villages, a town, or an area was sometimes held responsible for the misdeeds of one of its inhabitants. These stern measures were designed to discourage criminal behavior, as were other public punishments like crucifixion, impalement, dismemberment by oxen or carts pulling the body in opposite directions, boiling, dunking victims in water while they were tied up in bamboo mats, or cutting off their ears and noses. Indeed, this era marked the zenith of cruelty in the history of punishment in Japan.

B. *Han*-and-Village Feudalism
Early Edo Era, 1587–1742

The feudal system of the early modern period was significantly different from the *shōen*-style feudalism of the Middle Ages. We have already noted, for example, that the village had become the basic economic unit of the system. Likewise, the entire country was subdivided into *han*,* or *daimyō* domains. Each *han*, in turn, was comprised of villages. Hence, it is appropriate to refer to the feudalism of the early modern period as "*han*-and-village" feudalism.

1. The Status of Chief of the Warrior Houses
After Oda Nobunaga's assassination in 1582, Toyotomi Hideyoshi was able to unify Japan. He was of humble birth, however, and, lacking a Minamoto pedigree, could not legitimately assume the post of *sei-i-tai-shōgun*. Instead, he was formally adopted by a Kyoto courtier, Konoe Sakihisa, and thus became qualified for appointment as *kanpaku*. Hideyoshi became the virtual ruler of the entire country, and while he did not become *shōgun*, he was for all intents and purposes the chief of the warrior houses (*buke no tōryō*).

Hideyoshi died in 1598, and his family was soon obliged to pass the reins of government to his most powerful ally and retainer, Tokugawa Ieyasu. Ieyasu established hegemony over other *daimyō* with victory at the battle of Sekigahara, and was appointed

---

* The term *han* was initially used by scholars to describe *daimyō* domains; the word came into official usage only in the latter part of the Edo era.

shōgun by the emperor in 1603. This appointment merely confirmed the fact that Ieyasu had become the chief of the warrior
houses; it was not, in itself, a prerequisite for the establishment of
his *bakufu*. Nevertheless, it was advantageous for Ieyasu to be ele-
vated to a status higher than the heirs of the Toyotomi family,
and the title of *shōgun* and other court titles from the ancient source
of political legitimacy—the imperial court—accomplished this
purpose. Ieyasu's heirs invariably conformed with the precedent
he set in obtaining imperial recognition as *shōgun*, and in this
way they resembled the *bakufu* leaders of the Kamakura and
Muromachi eras.

After the outbreak of the Ōnin War in 1467, most of the *honjo*
and *kuge* domains were expropriated by the warriors, and under
Hideyoshi and the Tokugawa chiefs, all lands belonging to temples
and shrines, as well as those belonging to the *daimyō*, were regranted in fief after being surveyed and assessed (their assessed
value being expressed in terms of annual rice production). By the
beginning of the Edo era, consequently, all lands in the country
had become warrior domains. The total assessed land in the
country, at the close of the Edo era, amounted to about 30
million *koku* (one *koku* equals about four bushels, in this case, of
estimated annual rice yield). The *bakufu*, however, controlled only
seven million of this directly, 2.6 or 2.7 million of which had been
awarded as stipendary grants to its direct retainers, *hatamoto* or
gokenin. Most of the remaining land in Japan, producing twenty-
two or twenty-three million *koku*, was allotted to the *daimyō*, and
they were formally charged with administration of their domains.
Naturally, the *bakufu* reserved the authority to supervise the administration of the various *daimyō* and also retained the right to
establish nationwide regulations when necessary regarding
currency, transportation, and weights and measures. However,
the *daimyō* enjoyed virtual autonomy within his domain, for
bakufu law did not normally apply directly to the people therein.

The Tokugawa *shōgun* represented Japan in relations with
foreign countries, but after 1637, intercourse with all nations
except the Netherlands, China (on an unofficial basis), and Korea
was formally prohibited, and Japan entered a period of national
isolation (*sakoku*).

The chief of the warrior houses was extremely careful to curb any challenge to his prerogatives from the court. In 1615, for example, the *bakufu* issued the *Kinchū narabini kuge sho-hatto*, a set of strict rules regulating the activities of the throne and court nobility so as to prevent a revival of their power. Particular care was also taken to prevent any alliance between the court and dissident *daimyō*. The domains allotted to the court were limited at first to 20,000 *koku* but later raised to 30,000 *koku*. The emperor was empowered to do little other than bestow ranks, titles, and honors, affix era names, and set calendar dates, and even then only when the *bakufu* requested him to do so. In time the *bakufu* assumed the prerogative of granting ranks and titles to warriors, and the emperor was asked to issue an oral confirmation of such grants after they were made. The historical scholars of the Edo era expended considerable effort devising justification for the *bakufu* monolopoly of authority which in ancient times had been exercised by the emperor alone. The orthodox theory held that the *bakufu* had been entrusted with the tasks of government by the throne, or acted as the emperor's representative in actual administration and politics. During the first half of the Edo era, these concerns did not pose any serious problems, and were confined to the realm of scholarly speculation. Only later did they become a a point of argument for those who sought to undermine the authority of the Tokugawa *bakufu*.

2. Hideyoshi's Cadastral Survey (Taikō Kenchi)

The medieval land system was completely reformed by Toyotomi Hideyoshi when he had the *taikō kenchi* compiled. Land surveys had been conducted prior to Hideyoshi's ascent to power; but they were not actually field surveys. Oda Nobunaga's survey, for instance, consisted merely of requiring landholders to submit their ledgers (*sashidashi*) to the inspecting officials. To compile the *taikō kenchi*, however, Hideyoshi dispatched his officials to all localities in Japan, and they were required to make land registers on the basis of actual surveys of the land. Furthermore, his surveyors took the village (*mura*) as the basic economic unit and reorganized the entire country into village units. In the process, local communities hitherto designated as *shō, gō, ho, ri,* and others were abolished and replaced with *mura*.

Hideyoshi's survey also ended the old practice of dividing the rights to land among a variety of *shiki* holders. In fact, the importance of *shiki* rights had gradually declined with the usurpation of *shōen* lands by the warriors, and Hideyoshi's survey was only the final blow to the *shiki* system. The proprietary rights (*ryōshu-shiki*) to the *shōen* had long since been absorbed into the prerogatives of the provincial chiefs, and *shiki* belonging to *shōen* officials also disappeared. The only *shiki* which still survived in many places were those of landowners (*jinushi-shiki*) and cultivators (*saku-shiki*).

Where two different people held these rights, there was a growing tendency for one to purchase the rights of the other, but before Hideyoshi's survey the two often coexisted. The surveyors of the *taikō kenchi* recognized only one of these people as the responsible holder (*nauke-nin*) of a tract of land, and recorded his name with the land in the registers. They selected the person actually cultivating the land, who was responsible for paying the land tax (*nengu*). While the rights of the *nauke-nin* derived solely from the land survey, they were preeminent and could not be challenged on the basis of rights held by others prior to the survey. His rights were called *saku-shiki*, but they were not cultivation rights as presurvey *saku-shiki* had been. Indeed, the *saku-shiki* recognized by Hideyoshi's surveyors corresponded closely to the rights of land ownership (*jinushi-ken*) established in the Edo era.

The *taikō kenchi* and other land surveys established clear guidelines for levying taxes. Hideyoshi abolished the special *shōen* exemptions from taxation and entry by taxation officials, and thereby destroyed the remains of the *shōen* system. All land was publicly declared to be under direct government control (or to be a *daimyō* domain by virtue of government control). The *bakufu* and *daimyō* became landholders (*ryōshu*) with the official right to tax and administer their lands (*ryōchi-ken*). As we have noted, the surveys also created the *saku-shiki*, a private property right in arable land which was the counterpart of the *ryōchi-ken* held by the lords.

Hideyoshi also sought to obtain surplus land for his vassals by using the land survey to standardize the field system (which varied from district to district) and correcting inequities in the extraction of revenue from fief holdings. The *masu* measure of rice, which varied in value in different areas, was now replaced by the standard *kyōmasu* measure. Similarly, land had previously been assessed in terms of either its *kandaka* (the tax amount in cash that could be levied on it), or its *kokudaka* (rice productivity); after the land surveys, only the latter standard of land value was recognized. Measures of length and area were also standardized. The old *ken* measure of length, which previously equalled six *shaku* and five *sun*, was now shortened to six *shaku* and three *sun*. While one square *ken* was still regarded as the equivalent of one *bu*, it became standard practice to refer to one square *ken* as one *tsubo*. On the other hand, the *tan*, which previously comprised 360 *bu*, was now changed to 300 *bu*. Standard equivalents were established for the *cho*, *tan*, *se*, and *bu*, with thirty *bu* equaling one *se* and ten *se* making one *tan*.*

In short, the *taikō kenchi* wrought radical changes in the land system which had prevailed in the Middle Ages. Its greatest importance as a land reform was that it now granted ownership rights (*saku-shiki* or *jinushi-ken*) to the one person who tilled the land with responsibility for paying taxes on it. In other words, it denied overtenants the right to collect cultivation fees. We have already indicated that the confiscation of lands privately owned by the emperor and influential families, achieved through the Taika Reform, was the first great agrarian reform in Japanese history. The second great land reform occurred when the *taikō kenchi* abolished the rights of absentee landowners.

---

* The system of measurements applied to the taxing process varied widely before Hideyoshi's time. The system of volume measurement he adopted was:

1 *gō*	.1804 litres
10 *gō* = 1 *shō*	1.804 litres
10 *shō* = 1 *to*	18.04 litres
10 *to* = 1 *koku*	180.4 litres

The measurements of length and area used in land surveys also varied before Hideyoshi's time. One of the more common systems employed was:

10 *sun* = 1 *shaku*	30.3 centimeters
6 *shaku* 5 *sun* = 1 *ken*	1.97 meters
1 square *ken* = 1 *bu*	3.879 sq. meters
360 *bu* = 1 *tan*	1,396.4 sq. meters
10 *tan* = 1 *chō*	13,964 sq. meters

The system introduced by Hideyoshi was as follows:

10 *sun* = 1 *shaku*	30.3 centimeters
6 *shaku* 3 *sun* = 1 *ken*	1.909 meters
1 square *ken* = 1 *tsubo* (1 *bu*)	3.644 sq. meters
30 *tsubo* = 1 *se*	109.32 sq. meters
10 *se* = 1 *tan*	1,093.2 sq. meters
10 *tan* = 1 *chō*	10,932 sq. meters

3. Han-and-Village Feudalism

a) Feudalism under Toyotomi Hideyoshi. The *yori-oya* style of leader-retainer relationships and the village-*onkyū* system of the *sengoku* era were consolidated by Hideyoshi, establishing the basis of the feudalism of the early modern period. One of Hideyoshi's most significant measures in this regard was his policy of differentiating between warriors and cultivators. This policy was the outgrowth of developments which had taken place in the *sengoku* era. Before that, warriors remained in their villages and worked the land except for periods of warfare when they were summoned to battle; during the *sengoku* era, it became increasingly common for them to remain permanently in the castle-towns (*jōkamachi*) to guard their master's castle. This tendency promoted a growing distinction between farmers and warriors, which Hideyoshi institutionalized in 1588 by ordering a "sword-hunt" (*katanagari*) to disarm the nation's peasantry. Those who worked the land were permanently classified as peasants and were forbidden to abandon farming. Then, in 1591, Hideyoshi forbade warriors in the castle-towns to engage in mercantile or agrarian pursuits and forbade peasants to become wage-earners or merchants. It was decreed that warriors constituted a political ruling class distinct from peasants, merchants, or craftsmen, and were obliged to remain in their castle-towns.

The legal security of landholding rights was, in one sense, considerably strengthened by Hideyoshi's policies, but in another sense it became extremely tenuous. On the one hand, his surveys established that peasants enjoyed the rights to certain lands. Land values were expressed in terms of *taka* (*daka*), an assessment of the amount of unpolished rice the land might yield in an ordinary harvest. The total value of lands held by a village was termed the *mura-daka*, and this unit was used to express the value of a village granted personally to a *daimyō* as part of his domain. Since the fief was personally granted by the supreme political authority, who monopolized the right to determine legitimate landholding, *daimyō* who received fiefs from Hideyoshi could be secure in the knowledge that no other claims of ownership to their land would be recognized as legitimate. Under the Kamakura *bakufu*, the warrior-proprietor receiving confirmation of land from Yoritomo was secure only in possession (*chigyō*) of the land. His right to it was not inviolate, and if the true landholder appeared to challenge his claim to the land, he faced the danger of losing it. Hence, the *daimyō* under Hideyoshi enjoyed far greater security of landholding than his Kamakura ancestors. But while his position *vis-à-vis* rival claimants to the land was strengthened, he held the land purely at the discretion of Hideyoshi. Since the domain was granted to him personally, it was not legally heritable. When the *daimyō* died, the land formally reverted to Hideyoshi. While Hideyoshi customarily regranted the land to the *daimyō*'s heir, he was not obliged to do so.

b) *Han-and-Village Feudalism*. Through the development of strong institutions, Tokugawa Ieyasu was able to control and stabilize the roughly structured feudal system developed by Hideyoshi. Ieyasu took the decentralized feudal system of the *sengoku* era and placed it under strong overall controls, giving birth to a new system which has been called "decentralized feudalism under overall central control" (*tōsei-teki bunken-teki hōkensei*). The *shōgun-daimyō* relationship bore some resemblance to the ties binding the emperor and *uji* chieftains together in the archaic period; however, while the earlier ties were based on blood lineage (*shizoku-teki*), those of the Edo era were purely feudal (*hōken-teki*). Thus, as we called the political order of the archaic period a "nation of *uji* groups held together" (*shizoku-teki tōgō kokka*), we regard the Edo political order as "unified feudalism" (*tōgō-teki hōkensei*).

Under the Edo *bakufu*, *han* and village evolved from *sengoku* prototypes, and *bakufu* laws established a new terminology to describe the two critical elements of the feudal system. The relationship between *yori-oya* and *yori-ko* was no longer described by those words, but instead by the word *shihai* ("control"). Instead of the term *onkyū*, *bakufu* law increasingly used the term *fujo* ("assistance") to describe the benefices bestowed by superiors on their subordinates. The appearance of these new terms suggested that Edo feudalism had evolved from a dual to a single, hierarchically structured system, rooted in a leader-retainer relationship of control by superiors and the compensation of subordinates in the form of income from village production. This system contrasts sharply with the *shōen* feudalism of the Middle Ages. *Han*, or *daimyo* domains, now occupied the entire country (the *bakufu* itself may be seen as a kind of super-*daimyō*), and each of these was composed of village units. Although it is true that the term *han*, meaning a *daimyō* domain, was a scholarly invention not in official use until the end of the Edo period, the term *han* is used here to characterize this distinctive feudalism of the early modern period, which will now be examined more closely by an analysis of the concepts of *shihai* (control) and *fujo* (assistance).

"Control": *The Leader-Retainer Relationship*. A massive hierarchical system of control among warriors was created in the Edo era. At its apex stood the current leader of the Tokugawa house, the reigning *shōgun*. Immediately below him were his direct retainers (*kashin*), who were ranked in decreasing order of importance as *daimyō*, *hatamoto*, *gokenin*, and *kōke*; immediately under them stood their own direct retainers. All of the *shogun's kashin* with ranks from *daimyō* to *gokenin* were under the control of *bakufu* officials in peace and war. Hence, their relationship as subordinate retainers to the *shōgun* or chief of the warrior houses is known as a leader-retainer relationship of control (*shihai-teki shūjūsei*): they communicated *bakufu* orders to their subordinates and transmitted requests from their followers to higher authorities. In short, they held an intermediary position in the hierarchy. This hierarchy became a chain of command under wartime conditions. The relationship between the leader and his subordinate was a strong feudal one, evidenced in the honor felt at being able to die in battle in defense of the leader.

The direct retainers of the *shōgun* who held fiefs exceeding 10,000 *koku* enjoyed the status of *daimyō* and were under the control of the *rōjū* (senior councilors) of the Tokugawa *bakufu*. While their number varied during the Edo era, it was generally around 270. The fiefs of most *daimyō* did not exceed 100,000 *koku* in value, and only sixteen held fiefs exceeding 300,000 *koku*. Their position of subordination to the Tokugawa house was originally determined by the military supremacy of Ieyasu's forces, and it was formally confirmed when he was granted the title of *shōgun* in 1603. They themselves swore oaths confirming his leadership in 1611–12, and each succeeding *shōgun* exacted similar oaths from the *daimyō*. The *daimyō* were also periodically required to attend oral recitations of the rules governing warrior conduct, the *Buke sho-hatto*. Among the services they were to provide the *shōgun*, none was more important than to fight on his behalf in times of war. They had to reside in Edo periodically, and were also obliged to be in attendance at his castle at regular intervals and on extraordinary occasions as well. The *bakufu* developed a carefully constructed system of restraints to control the *daimyō*. Strategically located areas of the country were placed directly under *bakufu* control, or were entrusted as domains to *shinpan daimyō* (members of the Tokugawa family) and *fudai daimyō* (Ieyasu's followers since well before the battle of Sekigahara). Other *daimyō*, whose loyalty to the Tokugawa house was of a later date and hence not as trustworthy, called *tozama daimyō*, were relegated to domains in distant localities. All *daimyō* were required to maintain a close watch on each other, and to spend every other year in actual residence at the *shōgun*'s capital in Edo. This system of alternate residence (*sankin-kōtai*) permitted a *daimyō* to spend one out of every two years in his own domain but required him to leave his wife and children in Edo as hostages while he was out of the capital. The regular pilgrimages between the respective domains and Edo involved enormous expenditures for the *daimyō*, thus enabling the *bakufu* to limit their economic power. They were obliged also to contribute to the *bakufu*'s repairs of Edo castle and other public works, which further drained their financial resources. At the same time, however, such measures fostered the creation of excellent transportation and communication networks throughout the country and the growth of Edo as a major urban center. In turn, these developments stimulated the growth of a commercial economy, which ultimately undermined the very foundation of the feudal system.

A *daimyō* used many of the *bakufu*'s methods to control his own retainers. His retainers, or "indirect vassals" (*baishin*), were in the same subordinate relationship to him that he was to the *shōgun*, but the *daimyō* required all of his vassals, direct and lower, to live in his castle-town on a permanent basis.

The *hatamoto* and *gokenin* were direct retainers of the *shōgun*, but their fiefs were valued at less than 10,000 *koku*. They were under direct control of the junior councilors (*waka-doshiyori*) of the *bakufu*. The *hatamoto* were distinguished from *gokenin* in that they enjoyed the right of audience (*omemie*) with the *shōgun* and the *gokenin* did not. Both groups were required to live in Edo, and a special code of behavior for them (the *Shoshi hatto*) was established under Iemitsu, the third Tokugawa *shōgun*. However, Tsunayoshi, the fifth *shōgun*, abolished this code, and they became subject to the regulations of the *Buke sho-hatto* thereafter. A survey in 1722 estimated the number of *hatamoto* at over 5,000, while the number of *gokenin* exceeded 17,000. Although none of them had the requisite 10,000 *koku* to qualify as *daimyō*, some were nevertheless required to participate in *sankin-kōtai* and placed under the control of the *rōjū*, or councilors. Those so designated were called *kōtai-yoriai*.

A special ranking of direct retainers of the *shōgun* were the *kōke*. These were families which, since the *sengoku* era, had been renowned for their mastery of ceremony. The *bakufu* utilized them in the ceremonies of its own administration and afforded them special privileges in return for their services.

"Assistance" from Village Production: The Tokugawa *shōgun* extended assistance, or payment (*fujo*), to his *hatamoto* and *gokenin* in two different forms. They might receive fiefs (*jikata* or *chigyō*), or they might receive direct payments in rice. Far more retainers received rice payments than fiefs, but the actual value of payment by fief grants far exceeded the total value of rice payments. For example, a 1722 survey revealed that roughly 2,700 *hatamoto* and *gokenin* had received fiefs, while about 20,000 had received rice payments. The productive value of the fiefs granted, however, totaled 2,640,000 *koku* while the outlay of rice payments totaled 550,000 *koku*. Most "assistance" granted by Edo was therefore in the form of land grants, or *jikata*, and the same seems to have been true of the *daimyō* domains as well.

Enfeoffed land granted as "assistance" was generally called "private land" (*shiryō*). This term differentiated such land from land held directly by the *bakufu* (*goryō* or, popularly, *tenryō*) and the holdings of temples and shrines (*jisharyō*). The *shiryō* category included the *daimyō* domains, or *ryōbun*, the *hatamoto* domains, or *chigyōsho*, and *kyūchi*, lands allotted to *gokenin*. *Daimyō* were called "lords" (*ryōshu*) of their domains, while *hatamoto* and *gokenin* were termed "superintendants" (*jitō*) of theirs. As such, these authorities constituted the ruling elite, superior to farmers, artisans, and merchants. Temples and shrines might, depending on the case, be considered as either lords or supervisors of their holdings.

Shiryō of all kinds was evaluated in terms of its total estimated rice yield in *koku*, called the *kusa-daka* or *chigyō-daka*. This in turn was calculated by adding up the assessed standard yield of each village making up the fief, or *mura-daka*. *Bakufu* vassals, when granted "assistance" in the form of domains, were actually given *fujo* to the value of so many *koku* from a series of specified villages which they were permitted to hold as *ryōchi*. In fact, they did not receive the entire production of the land they held as fiefs, but only the taxes (*nengu*) paid by the cultivators. Thus, if the tax rate were 50 percent, the fief-holder actually received for his own use an amount totaling 50 percent of the assessed *chigyō-daka* of his fief. Since he had to support his retainers from this amount, his own share of the income from the land was still smaller.

While surveyors took great pains to insure the accuracy of their assessments of *mura-daka*, the actual production of village lands naturally changed between one survey and another. Consequently, the *mura-daka* figures and the *chigyō-daka* figure based on them were usually at variance with the actual revenue derived from the land.

During this period, most villagers were land-owning cultivators (*hon-byakushō*). The later practice of one person's obtaining owner-ship rights to many plots of land was still comparatively rare, and the economic condition of the villages as objects of feudal grants of "assistance" was generally sound.

A fief ordinarily consisted of one solid tract of land, but at times it also included widely separated parcels of land called *tobichi*. Most of the *hatamoto* and *gokenin* fiefs were located in the Kantō region, where it was not uncommon for tax revenues from one vil-lage to be divided among several fief-holders.

Although a *daimyō* did not have to pay taxes to the *shōgun*, the lands he received as *fujo* grants carried with them a number of feudal obligations. As a wartime service (*gun-yaku*), he had to bring with him into the *shōgun*'s camp a number of men, horses, and weapons commensurate with the size of his fief. In addition, he had other responsibilities which included supporting *bakufu* public work projects and providing guards and firemen for Edo Castle. The initial inclination of the *bakufu* after the battle of Sekigahara was to eliminate as many *daimyō* as possible, and more than 120, with fiefs totaling 12 million *koku*, were in fact stripped of their positions before a rebellion by Yui Shōsetsu in 1651 persuaded the *bakufu* to relax this policy.

We have noted that in addition to granting fiefs, "assistance" also took the form of outright payments of rice to retainers. This rice was stored in warehouses (*kura*) and was thus called *kuramai*.

It was distributed primarily to *gokenin* of lower rank. The rice was referred to by a variety of other terms as well. For example, periodical (seasonal) rice payments to retainers were called *kirimai* and consisted of a certain number of *koku* or "bales" (*hyō*). (One bale equaled three *to* five *shō*, or .35 *koku*.) Since rice in the *bakufu* warehouses in the Asakusa section of Edo was originally received from villages as tax-rice, it was called *nengu-mai*. Retainers received their *kirimai* payments in kind (*nengu-mai*) and partly in cash. The rice could also be considered "allowance rice" (*fuchi-mai*) for a certain number of persons. One man's allowance (*ichinin-buchi*) amounted to five *gō* of rice daily. The *hatamoto* and *gokenin* usually had to sell some of their rice for cash in order to purchase other commodities. Edo merchants who handled the sale of warriors' rice were called *fudasashi*, and they became an important element in the commercial structure of the economy.

Once the elaborate feudal system of the early modern period had been established, the *bakufu* made every effort to preserve it. A vital factor in the successful maintenance of the system was the payment of taxes on the product of village lands. The *bakufu* held that the surest way to preserve the economic viability of villages as the source of taxation was to prevent social and economic change in the countryside. Efforts were therefore made to keep the money economy from intruding upon the natural, self-sufficient economic units which formed the basis of the feudal system. Even at its beginning, the Edo *bakufu* realized that the money economy could not be ignored, but it never acted positively to encourage it out of fear of endangering its own supremacy. The monetary aspects of the economy were simply accepted as inevitable, to be occasionally exploited as circumstances warranted.

By the Genroku era (1688–1704), when the bourgeois culture centering on Osaka reached its height, the reserves of wealth accumulated in Ieyasu's time were so depleted that the *bakufu* was forced to resort to such expedients as debasing its own coinage. Yoshimune, who served as the eighth *shōgun* from 1716 to 1745, reversed this policy, and strengthened the *bakufu's* financial position by emphasizing the virtues of temperance and frugality. His approach demonstrated that the *bakufu* could still remain economically viable if it followed sound fiscal policies; but by the early nineteenth century, it had become too weak to be resuscitated by the fiscal policies which had worked effectively for Yoshimune.

The principal instrument for preserving the supremacy of the *bakufu* and the status system was Confucianism. This ideology originated in the fifth century B.C. in China, and was aimed at rehabilitating an already declining feudal system. While it was not lacking in universally valid principles, it supported a nationwide hierarchy of status consisting of, from top to bottom, the son of haeven, the various lords, the grandees, the gentlemen, and the commoners. Its personal ethic was based on the subordination of son to father, younger to elder brother, wife to husband, and junior to senior. As applied by the *bakufu*, it was imbued with the status distinction between commoners and *samurai*, who were identified as "gentlemen." This proved to be a wonderfully effective technique for creating a strongly entrenched feudal order.

There are two other observations which should be made about the Edo feudal system. First, while *daimyō* were virtually autonomous rulers in their domains, they were also regarded as the chief local officers of the *bakufu*. This fact is clear from the regulations of the *Buke sho-hatto* of 1615, which enjoined them to select competent men to staff their administrations. Another indication of their status as regional officers of the *bakufu* appeared in the type of *ritsuryō*-style titles they received. While such appellations as *Awaji-no-kami* ("governor of Awaji") and *Echizen-no-kami* ("governor of Echizen") were largely honorific, they conveyed a sense of the local administrative posts with which they had been associated in the past. This facet of *daimyō* status was of such importance to the *bakufu* that maladministration and improper exercise of power by *daimyō* elicited the same punishments as did rebellions and breaches of loyalty. In either case, a *daimyō* could suffer a reduction in the size of his fief, enforced removal from his lands to another fief, or the dissolution of his house.

Another vital factor in the successful maintenance of the feudal system was class stability. In order to maintain the special position of the military, it was considered essential to adopt a system of rigid class distinctions.

A final noteworthy feature of Edo feudalism was the clear distinction that was made between the public nature of the feudal lord's rights to the land (*ryōchi-ken*) and the private property rights of the commoner (*shoji-ken*). The *daimyō*'s rights to his fief were supported by a written *bakufu* certificate confirming the size of the fief and the villages included in it. If the fief was less than 100,000 *koku*, this certificate took the form of a "vermilion-seal letter" (*shuin-jō*); fiefs exceeding 100,000 *koku* were confirmed by certificates with the *shōgun*'s written monogram (*hanmotsu*). On the other hand, the land-owning rights of commoners (*shoji*) rested on the survey land registers, as discussed earlier. The sources of legitimate rights were thus entirely separate.

The rights of *daimyō* and commoner to the land were differentiated in other respects as well. The *daimyō*'s right to the land (*ryōchiken*) technically referred only to his right to receive its proceeds. Historically, however, this right was understood to include administrative and judicial rights as well, which were not included in the property rights of the commoner. However, the commoner was entitled to hold his land rights in perpetuity (*eitai no katoku*), implying their hereditary character; *daimyō* held their land only personally and technically could not pass it on to their heirs without the consent of the *shōgun*.

As we observed earlier, the hereditary nature of commoners' property rights was the central concept in the general notion of property rights. While private property ownership as defined by the *taikō kenchi* thus paved the way for modern concepts, in other respects it was directly related to the concept of rights to property prevalent in the Middle Ages. For example, unlike modern property rights, the rights of the Edo property holder were based solely on the land survey, and could be forfeited as a result of later surveys. Furthermore, if the land had to be mortgaged, both mortgagee and mortgager were held to be the landowner (*jinushi*) and the rights of each were called *shoji* (ownership). Thus, property rights remained divisible during the Edo era, as they had been earlier.

4. The Control Structure

While Hideyoshi did not formally establish a *bakufu*, his government did not in fact differ significantly from the *bakufu* form. He divided political responsibility among his five most important retainers and appointed five elders (*toshiyori*), including Tokugawa Ieyasu, to serve as a supreme advisory council. He stationed deputies (*daikan*) in lands directly under his supervision (*kurairi*) and special representatives to serve him as commissioners (*bugyō*) in the cities of Osaka and Sakai. At the level of local administration, he standardized all units below the *gun* level as *mura*, and sought to control murder, robbery, and theft by organizing warriors into squads of five men (*samurai gonin-gumi*) and commoners into ten-man units (*genin jūnin-gumi*).

The Edo *bakufu* was remarkably simple in its bureaucratic structure, being little more than an enlargement of the administration the Tokugawa had established in the province of Mikawa. Both the conference system and the system of rotating guard duties on a monthly basis (*tsukiban-sei*) were also well developed. Originally, the most important *bakufu* officials were the elders. Senior councilors (called *toshiyori* until the middle of the eighteenth century, and *rōjū* thereafter) served in the *shōgun*'s inner offices (*goyō-beya*) and outranked the junior councilors (*waka-doshiyori*). When the occasion demanded, a regent (*tairō*) was appointed for the *shōgun*, but this was only a temporary post. From Tsunayoshi's reign as *shōgun*, the chamberlains of the *shōgun*'s castle (*osoba-yōnin*) also became a political force to be reckoned with. A Chief Censor (*ōmetsuke*) and censorate (*metsuke*) maintained constant surveillance over the activities of *daimyō* and *hatamoto*, respectively, and the latter performed peace-keeping duties within Edo castle. The most important *bakufu* officials in the realm of civil administration were the *jisha-bugyō*, *machi-bugyō*, and *kanjō-bugyō*—more simply, the "three commissioners" (*sanbugyō*). The *jisha-bugyō* handled matters relating to shrines, temples, and priests. The *kanjō-bugyō* had charge of *bakufu* finances, as well as all legal and administrative affairs in *bakufu* lands. The *machi-bugyō* dealt with the legal and administrative affairs of Edo and its citizens. Any lawsuit involving these officials was decided by the judicial council (*hyōjōsho*), which comprised the *sanbugyō*.

The military command system under Hideyoshi was not especially noteworthy, but that under the Tokugawa was a different matter. The peacetime political system could be transformed immediately into a military command system when war occurred. If the *bakufu* was mobilized for battle, the *rōjū* assumed command of the *daimyō* and the *wakadoshiyori* commanded the *hatamoto*; the Chief Censor (*ō-metsuke*) monitored the *daimyō*, and the censorate (*metsuke*) monitored the *hatamoto*. In peacetime, the military organization of the *bakufu* was essentially a guard system (*bangata*).

There were five grades of guards, *ōban, shoinban, koshō-gumiban, shinban,* and *kojūnin-gumi.* Their main duty was to guard the castles of Edo and Osaka and serve as guards in the *shōgun*'s retinue. The process of becoming a guard (*banshū*) was called *ban'iri. Hatamoto* and *gokenin* considered it a great honor to be appointed guards and vied for the highest honor of appointment as chief of the *ōban* (*ōban-gashira*).

The most important local official in the *bakufu* system was the Kyoto *shoshidai,* who was responsible for policing the imperial palace and the imperial capital. The *shoshidai* also handled all ordinary *bakufu* dealings with the imperial family. In other important cities, *bugyō* were appointed as in Hideyoshi's time, and *daikan* were stationed throughout *bakufu* domains (*goryō*) to govern them. *Gundai* were appointed to govern particularly large areas of *bakufu* domains.

The administrative organizations of the *han* varied from place to place, but were generally patterned after the structure of the *bakufu* system. The *rōjū* of the *bakufu* found their *han* counterparts in the *karō,* while *chūrō* and *yōnin* were the *han* equivalents of the *waka-doshiyori* and *soba-yōnin* positions in the *bakufu. Daimyō* also appointed censors (*metsuke*) and had officers corresponding to the *san-bugyō* of the *bakufu.* Many also established *hyōjōsho* and *kuji-ba* to adjudicate lawsuits. They likewise appointed local officials called *kōri-bugyō* and *daikan,* in emulation of the *bakufu* system.

5. Villages and Cities

a) *Villages* (*Mura*). As we have seen, under Hideyoshi the units called *shō, gō, ho,* and *ri* were subsumed under the name *mura.* The village was a vital unit under Edo feudalism, in two senses. First, as we have indicated earlier, payments or "assistance" to subordinates were made in terms of the tax income from specific village units. Second, the village was an organized body of inhabitants and a standard administrative unit of land.

The population of the agrarian village was made up of landowning farmers (*hon-byakushō*) and landless (or "water-drinking") farmers (*mizunomi-byakushō*). In remote areas, there were other subordinate classes of landless peasants, remnants of the land system of the middle ages, who were called *nago* or *hikan;* they owed several days' annual labor service to the owners of land they cultivated in addition to rental in kind. Only land-owning farmers, however, had any legal standing in the village; hence, the village as a legal entity consisted only of *hon-byakushō* (sometimes called simply *hyakushō*). Land-owning farmers were in the majority at this time, and conditions in the agrarian village can be said to have been quite satisfactory.

Each village had its own offices for governing its internal affairs. The most important village officials (*mura-yakunin*) were the village headman (*nanushi* or *shōya*), the sub-headman (*kumi-gashira*), and the representative of the landowner (*hyakushō-dai*). These three officials were referred to collectively as the *murakata-san'yaku*. The headman was responsible for overseeing every aspect of village administration. He was assisted by four or five sub-headmen, while the *hyakushō-dai* served as village overseers. All village officials were responsible to the landowners for their actions, but they were also utilized by the *bakufu* and *daimyō* as intermediaries between the warrior administration and the village. Important matters affecting the interests of all villagers were decided at meetings of the village council (*mura-yoriai*). The council established rules governing village life, called *mura-gime* or *mura-gijōsho*, and those who broke these rules were often punished by ostracism from the affairs of the community (*mura-hachibu*). The village was collectively responsible for making tax payments on its citizens' lands to the feudal lord. It was the task of the village council to apportion the village's tax burden among the farmers and to collect the taxes for delivery to the government.

The Edo *bakufu* continued the practice of requiring villagers to organize themselves into neighborhood groups of five familes (*gonin-gumi*). These groups were originally used to discover traitors and followers of the prohibited Christian church. They had other policing functions as well, but eventually they evolved into mutual aid groups. The villagers themselves organized a number of other associations voluntarily. *Yui* and *moyai*, for example, were old labor organizations through which villagers helped each other in farming tasks, thatching roofs, conducting funerals and weddings, and so on. Other associations were organized for religious pilgrimages and for the performance of daily religious rites; these included the *Ise-kō, himachi-kō, nijūsan'ya-kō,* and others. There were also societies for mutual financial aid, such as the *tanomoshi-kō* and *mujin.*

b) Cities. Osaka served as Toyotomi Hideyoshi's principal base. However, he also placed the port town of Sakai under his direct control with an eye to profiting from the city's foreign trade. In Kyushu, he took control of Hakata and also seized Nagasaki, which had become a domain of the Jesuits. Ieyasu followed Hideyoshi's example of controlling the major cities directly. He protected them militarily and exempted them from land taxes. Similarly, many *daimyō* built their own castle-towns and made them the political and economic centers of their domains.

Many cities thus developed under the protection of political leaders while they retained some degree of autonomy in managing their affairs. Cities in the Edo era were of various types: castle-towns like Edo, Kanazawa, Nagoya, Sendai, and Hiroshima; commercial and industrial centers like Osaka (then called the "kitchen of Japan"), Sakai, Matsuzaka, and Kiryū; and port-towns like Nagasaki and Hakata. Urban centers also developed near large temples and shrines in Nara, Yamada, Nagano, Nikkō, and elsewhere, while Kyoto continued to thrive as the imperial capital and as a commercial and industrial center.

In the typical castle-town vassals lived in the area surrounding the *daimyō*'s residential castle, while merchants dwelt in another part of the city. Men of the same profession were obliged to live in the same quarters. Edo, the largest city and castle-town of the *bakufu*, constituted an administrative district under the control of the *machi-bugyō*. Various sub-districts (*machi*) within Edo were themselves minor semi-autonomous administrative units with their own officials (called *nanushi* and *tsuki-gyōji*). Residents (*chōnin*) of each sub-district were designated landowners (*jinushi*), house tenants (*tanagari*), or land tenants (*jikari*). The landowners and their agents (*yamori*) monopolized control of *machi* administration and thus functioned in roles analogous to the rural *murakata*.

6. The Financial System

The finances of the Toyotomi house were derived from three main sources: income from the land under its direct control (*kurairi-chi*), proceeds from mining operations, and profits from foreign trade. The latter two were the primary sources of the great wealth and power of the house, but the tax returns from the *kurairi-chi* were also significant. Indeed, the main objective of the *taikō kenchi* had been to set down clear guidelines for levying and collecting land taxes.

The chief financial resources of the Edo *bakufu* were tax returns from the land under its direct control (*goryō*), income from mines, *goyōkin* contributions (in theory, a kind of public bond subscribed to by wealthy urban citizens, but in fact frequently nothing more than forced donations), and profits from metallic currency debasement. The *bakufu* was, in essence, the biggest feudal lord in Japan, with direct control over lands producing about 4.5 million *koku* annually. Moreover, it did not bear the expenses of dual residence under the *sankin-kōtai* system as the *daimyō* did. Nevertheless, its financial burdens were extraordinarily heavy. It was responsible for governing the entire country and representing Japan in foreign affairs, but it had no special resources for these tasks. At times, special taxes (*kuniyaku*) and rice levies (*agemai*) were imposed on the domains, but by and large the costs of administering the country and its foreign relations had to be defrayed by ordinary *bakufu* income. Under Ieyasu and Hidetada, the first two Tokugawa *shōgun*, the *bakufu* accumulated enormous wealth from the spoils of war, foreign trade, and mining; this wealth paid its administrative expenses until the end of the seventeenth century. Thereafter, tax receipts remained the most important source of income with which the *bakufu* defrayed its regular expenses, but the profits gained from debasing metallic currency became a vital supplementary source of income.

The highest financial officer of the *bakufu* was called the "finance commissioner" (at first *kanjō gashira*, later *kanjō bugyo*). There were several types of taxation during the Edo era, including *honto-mononari, ko-mononari, taka-gakarimono, kuniyaku,* and *chishi*. The *honto-mononari* was a basic tax levied on surveyed lands (*taka-uke-chi*) in accordance with their official designated productive value (*taka*). The tax rate was originally 40 percent of the *taka*, although it was subsequently raised to 50 and commonly reached 60 percent in the *daimyō* domains. In time, more sophisticated methods for determining the tax rate were employed, such as the *kemi-hō* (by which the tax rate was determined on the basis of an annual survey of the harvest) and *jōmen-hō* (by which an appropriate tax rate was established on the basis of tax rates over several preceding years). While the rates were severe, taxpayers obtained some relief from the fact that land surveys were not always precise. Underestimations of *taka* values by as much as 20 percent were tolerated, so that the harvest formally subject to taxation was often considerably smaller than the actual harvest. One type of *ko-mononari* tax was imposed on lands which were not subject to the *honto-mononari* tax, and a second was levied on commercial and artisan producers in the form of exactions called *unjō* and *myōga*. The *taka-gakarimono* tax was a supplementary tax levied on *mura-daka* in addition to the *honto-mononari*. The purpose of the tax was to meet the expenses of transporting, feeding, and lodging official messengers and their horses. The *kuniyaku* was a levy imposed on specific territories in accordance with the production of their lands, to meet the expenses of engineering and riparian works, receiving delegations from Korea, and other extraordinary projects or events. *Chishi* was a tax on urban land.

During the early Edo era, the *bakufu*'s financial position was very strong because of the gold and silver acquired in war and the steadily rising profits from mining. By the end of the seventeenth century, however, the inheritance of precious metals had been largely consumed, and mining output had also declined, while *bakufu* expenditures continued to increase. The economic plight of the *bakufu* was experienced by most *daimyō* as well, and the penetration of a money economy posed a grave danger to the financial foundation of feudalism. Nevertheless, overall national land productivity (*kokudaka*) had risen from 18.5 million *koku* at the end of the sixteenth century to 30 million *koku* by the Kyōhō era (1716–1736), the time of the eighth Tokugawa *shōgun*, Yoshimune, providing ample resources for financial recovery. This cushion was the major factor underlying the signal success of the economic reforms undertaken by Yoshimune during that period.

Land surveys were carried out even after the beginning of the Edo era, but the *ken* measure of length was reduced to six *shaku*. In order to prevent the disintegration of the landholding patterns on which the tax system was based, the *bakufu* in 1643 prohibited the permanent sale of land held by landowners. Subsequently, this prohibition was applied to any land which had been officially surveyed and given a designated productive value. After 1673, restrictions were placed on the division of such lands among descendants. These varied from time to time: in 1713 it was ruled that no parcel distributed or retained in the family could be less than ten *koku* in assessed value or one *chō* in area. This rule was afterwards revised, but then was permanently restored in 1759.

7. The Judicial System and Penal Law

a) *The Judicial System.* The *daimyō* of the Edo era, like his *sengoku* predecessor, held judicial authority in criminal and civil cases involving the people of his domain, as long as the case did not involve the *bakufu* or other *daimyō*. Cases involving the *bakufu* or people from other domains fell under *bakufu* jurisdiction.

There were two types of *bakufu* court procedures. *Deiri-suji* was the procedure for adjudicating arguments of the plaintiff and defendant in court; it corresponded roughly to modern civil procedure. *Ginmi-suji* was criminal trial procedure. The court was authorized to summon suspects and try them. Confessions were a prerequisite for guilty verdicts, and the time-honored method of securing them by torture was followed in instances of serious offenses.

b) *Penal Law.* The harsh punitive spirit of the *sengoku* era persisted throughout the first half of the Edo era. Punishments were designed primarily to deter crime, and were therefore severe. The concept of punishment as a means of preventing crime was called *migori* (or *migorashi*) in the Edo era; the term conveys a sense of "public warning." This harsh spirit of penal enforcement was greatly modified during the second half of the Edo era.

C. The Decay of Tokugawa Feudalism
Late Edo Era, 1742–1858

The latter part of the early modern period (*kinsei*) witnessed the decline of feudalism. It provides us with a valuable case study of the process of feudal decay without the complicating instrusion of external influences. The period from 1742 to 1858 saw a continuity of the form and substance of *bakufu* rule characterizing the middle of the early modern period, but it was also a period of discontinuity in the sense that it marked the decay of the feudal system. It was also a time when the power of the common people—

particularly their economic power—grew considerably. While the growth of popular power was certainly a progressive social development, it was also, from the viewpoint of feudalism, a dangerous sign of decline.

As suggested earlier, the compilation of the *Kujikata Osadamegaki* provides a convenient line of demarcation between the middle and latter part of the early modern period. The compilation was ordered by Yoshimune and completed in 1742. It consisted of two volumes, the first containing eighty-one laws and the second listing regulations concerning the civil and penal codes. The second volume was not actually made public, since it was compiled solely for the reference of the three *bugyō* (*jisha, machi,* and *kanjō*) to use when they acted as *hyōjōsho* and advised the *rōjū*. The copy of the *Osadamegaki* which survives today is the product of several post-1742 revisions and consists of 103 articles. It is thus known commonly as the *Hyakkajō Osadamegaki* (One Hundred Articles). Before 1742 courts relied on individual laws and precedents in deciding cases, but thereafter the *Osadamegaki* served as the main guideline for court judgments. Precedents naturally remained important, and several official compilations were made of earlier cases (see, for example, the *Oshioki Reiruishu*). Still, the compilation of the *Kujikata Osadamegaki* clearly indicates a shifting of priorities in the policy of the *bakufu* with regard to civil officials in administration.

1. Emergence of Anti-bakufu and Anti-feudal Thought

During the middle part of the early modern period, it was argued (although largely on a theoretical level) that the chief of the warrior houses (*buke no tōryō*) governed as an imperial deputy and was entrusted with authority by the emperor. In the latter part of the period, however, a corollary to this theory emerged, holding that political power should be restored to its proper place, the imperial throne. Early proponents of this view included Takenouchi Shikibu, an adherent of Suika Shintoism, who urged his ideas on court nobles between 1751 and 1764 and was exiled by the *bakufu*. Yamagata Daini, Fujii Umon, and others were put to death in 1767 for advocating the restoration of imperial power and criticizing the legitimacy of *bakufu* authority. Other restorationists appeared toward the end of the century, including the "eccentrics"

Takayama Hikokurō and Gamō Kunpei (leader of the movement to repair imperial mausolea).

The two major intellectual stimulants to this "imperial loyalism" (*kinnō*) were the growing body of scholarship on Japanese history and the development of "national learning" (*kokugaku*). The most notable undertaking in Japanese historiography was, of course, the compilation of the *Dai-Nihonshi* (History of Great Japan) begun earlier in the Edo era under the patronage of the *daimyō* of the Mito *han*. In the latter part of the early modern period, this compilation promoted the emergence of a new group of thinkers—the so-called Mito school—concerned with the study of Japan's national essence (*kokutai*) and the concept of "rectification of names" (*seimei no gaku*). The chief members of the Mito school were Fujita Yūkoku, his son Fujita Tōko, and Aizawa Seishisai.

Somewhat before the Mito school achieved prominence, the classical scholar Kada no Azumamaro (1706–1761) laid the basis for "national learning" in Kyoto. He asserted that the purpose of studying the Japanese classics was not simply to gain linguistic and literary appreciation of ancient texts, but more fundamentally to discover, in the "ways of old" (*kodō*), the true ideals which the nation should pursue. His disciple, Kamo no Mabuchi, further developed Azumamaro's ideas and pursued the study of the "ways of old" revealed in the classics. Mabuchi's disciple, Motoori Norinaga (1730–1801), filled out the body of ideas that became known as "national learning," and his disciple, Hirata Atsutane, converted these teachings into a kind of religion.

The Mito school and "national learning" thus comprised a loyalist ideological reaction against the *bakufu*. Several other scholars espoused antifeudal ideas as well. While most advocated reform of the feudal system, Andō Shōeki—a physician from Akita—went so far as to denounce the feudal system altogether. In one of his tracts (*Jinen Shin'eidō*), Andō rejected the Confucian class structure and urged a return to a natural state of existence in which all men lived on the basis of their production. While Andō's ideas were remarkable for his time, and perhaps influenced by Dutch learning, they and the antifeudal ideas of other scholars had little influence on the process of destroying feudalism and the *bakufu*. Instead, it was the ideas of restorationism and loyalism that paved the way for the destruction of the feudal order.

2. Decay of Han-and-Village Feudalism

The decay of *han*-and-village feudalism may be observed in two contexts: first, in the personal nexus of leader-retainer relationships, and second, in the breakdown of the "assistance" (*fujo*) system of compensating retainers for their services.

a) Weakening Leader-Retainer Bonds. The feudal system required close and strong bonds between leaders and followers; but during the latter half of the Edo era, these bonds were gradually undermined. After the extermination of the Toyotomi family in 1615, war was virtually unknown under the Tokugawa *bakufu*. Since the primary service performed by retainers on behalf of their leaders was military, peace robbed them of their *raison d'être* and left them demoralized. The loss of military élan was evidenced clearly in the declining prestige of military positions and titles. *Hatamoto* and *gokenin*, who had once eagerly sought guard posts to perform military service, gradually developed a preference for official civil service positions (*yakukata*). The growing interest in civil affairs and declining importance of military service was indicative of the weakening military bond of feudal loyalty that had once been so intense. This trend continued despite the efforts by the eighth *shōgun*, Yoshimune, and the late eighteenth century *bakufu rōjū* Matsudaira Sadanobu to resuscitate martial spirit and élan.

The leader-follower bond was also undermined by retainers' loss of confidence in their leaders. Willingness to serve and die for the leader had originally been stimulated through the grant of fiefs or "assistance" to the retainer or by extending the promise of such grants in the future. By the latter half of the Edo era, the economic straits of the *daimyō* precluded the possibility of further grants. Indeed, *daimyō* sought to extricate themselves from insolvency by borrowing from their impoverished vassals, sometimes up to 50 percent of the value of the fiefs they had originally granted. It was therefore hardly surprising to find a weakening of the allegiance shown by subordinates to their masters. Meanwhile, the development of a money- and commodity-oriented economy also threatened the economic viability of *samurai* living on fixed incomes from their fiefs. Many were forced to pawn their swords—the "soul of the *samurai*." Others were obliged to start small businesses or take other employment in addition to their official duties in order to escape bankruptcy. Many, indeed, while retaining *samurai* status, were in fact at least as much merchants or craftsmen as warriors. *Samurai* with low rank developed a strong sense of resentment against the *daimyō* and high-ranking retainers who, even if incompetent, enjoyed large fief-holdings by virtue of their hereditary status. All of these conditions fostered the disintegration of the leader-follower bond vital to feudalism.

b) *Decline of "Assistance."* Edo feudalism also depended on the continued viability of the village as the foundation of the "assistance" system. In the early part of the Edo era, the agricultural villages served as the chief economic prop of the feudal system and subsidized the *samurai* with their growing expenditures. Yields from village fields grew steadily, generating higher tax returns and productive fiefs. For example, the nation's total *kokudaka*, which in 1598 stood at 18.5 million *koku*, increased dramatically to 25,780,-000 *koku* by the end of the seventeenth century. However, during the next century, the *kokudaka* increased less than 20 percent, to 30,430,000 *koku* in 1834, and most of this growth was directly attributable to the cultivation of new fields before 1735. Cultivation of new fields continued after that year, but total output remained relatively constant because older fields simultaneously degenerated. Without continued growth in production, the villages were less able to support the weight of a growing *samurai* class and its burgeoning expenses. Consequently, with the decline of the village economy, the economic base of feudalism itself began to crumble.

In large part, stagnation in agricultural production was due to shortages of material and manpower required for continuing agrarian prosperity. Rural impoverishment grew under the impetus of an advancing money economy in the countryside, coupled with excessive taxation, declining agrarian population, and the burden of a number of natural disasters. The penetration of a money economy into formerly self-sufficient villages was especially notable after the end of the seventeenth century. Farm products were increasingly sold on the market, and the proceeds from sales were used by farmers to purchase other commodities. The development of a money- and commodity-oriented economy inevitably led to higher consumption levels among the rural population, reducing the tax burden villages could bear. The *bakufu* tried vainly on many occasions to check this trend by exhorting the peasantry to live simply and avoid wasteful consumption and expenditure. Ultimately, the collapse of the village as a self-sufficient economic unit was to have profound implications on the stability of the peasantry as a class.

The money economy also created financial problems for the *daimyō*, who passed their difficulties along to the peasantry in the form of new and more exorbitant taxes and stricter enforcement of tax collection procedures. Peasants were at times forced to pay taxes from three to five years in advance in order to finance *daimyō* expenditures. The heavy burden of corvée labor (*sukegō*) was particularly deleterious to the economic solvency of the peasantry, leaving no surplus for investment in increased production. It was natural, then, that the rural population did not show any significant increase. In 1726 the population of commoners was about 26,540,000; in 1846, it was a little over 26,900,000, a gain of less than 3 percent in over 120 years. Besides famines and epidemics, population was held down by the practice of abortion and infanticide, and the agricultural sector was particularly affected by the large numbers of persons drifting into the cities. The penetration of the money economy into the villages brought about sharpened class divisions within the peasantry itself, so that some villagers were in fact engaged in commerce or manufacture rather than agriculture. As already noted, the demands of the *daimyō* for corvée labor taxed the agricultural labor resources even further.

Earthquakes, storms, droughts, floods, and other natural disasters wreaked havoc on agricultural life and production. Besides the lack of reserves already mentioned, inadequate transportation facilities and the feudally organized regional economy meant that when a natural disaster occurred, famine was almost inevitable. Conditions of starvation in northern Honshu during the famines of the eighteenth and early nineteenth centuries, for example, defy description. Villages struck by these famines could not easily recover, and even disasters of a lesser magnitude seriously impeded the growth of agricultural production.

The two salient signs of feudal decay during the late Edo era, thus, were the weakening of the leader-retainer bond and the declining viability of the village as the economic foundation of the feudal "assistance" system. In conjunction with these trends, grants from *daimyō* to their retainers shifted increasingly away from grants of enfeoffed land (*ryōchi*) in favor of rice stipends (*kuramai*).

Even in earlier times grants of *kuramai* had been given, but they now occupied a much larger share of the "assistance" given to vassals; this meant that the warriors were becoming a salaried class. Commercialized and professionalized, they lost their character as feudal retainers.

Under these conditions, the *han* lost their financial self-sufficiency and were forced to borrow from the merchants. The practice of borrowing became universal, and the need to sustain the feudal system with funds from the non-feudal sector shows the extent of its deterioration. It also meant the erosion of the power of the warriors and of the class system in which they ranked above peasants, artisans, and merchants.

3. Conditions in the Han

Bakufu officials took a variety of steps to forestall the gradual disintegration of the feudal economy. Between 1767 and 1786, the chamberlain Tanuma Okitsugu and his son Okitomo implemented a policy of alliance with wealthy merchants in order to draw upon their wealth in solving the *bakufu's* financial problems, but they failed. Matsudaira Sadanobu, one of the senior councilors under the *shōgun* Ienari, made a concerted attempt to resuscitate the administration through a policy of austerity during the Kansei period (1789–1801), but he too was doomed to failure. Indeed, shortly after Sadanobu's reforms had been discarded, Ienari (now retired) reversed this approach and abandoned most controls on consumption and expenditure. After his death, senior councilor Mizuno Tadakuni instituted anew the retrenchment approach to *bakufu* finance; but his policies, known collectively as the Tempō reforms of 1841, were too harsh and ended in failure. About ten years later, the *bakufu* was suddenly confronted with the appearance of Commodore Perry's "black ships," and in 1858 it was obliged to open the country to diplomatic and commercial intercourse, a step which hastened its own demise.

Most *han* experienced economic problems equal to or surpassing those of the *bakufu*. Although their economic foundation lay in the natural economy of the agrarian village, they were inevitably affected by the penetration of the money and commodity economy, and they experienced severe economic distress after the end of the seventeenth century. The *daimyō* were especially pressed by the economic burdens of the *sankin-kōtai* system and the expenses of living in Edo, which often consumed over half of their incomes. *Daimyō* sought to increase their incomes by raising the tax rate, borrowing from their vassals' fiefs, encouraging the cultivation of new fields, stimulating and controlling the sale and use of goods and foodstuffs produced in their domains, granting monopolies, issuing their own paper currency, and extracting contributions from their wealthy subjects. Many of these measures implied tacit recognition of the money economy by the *daimyō*. At the beginning of the period, some, like Hosokawa Shigekata of Higo and Uesugi Harunori of Yonezawa, were renowned for their successful reform programs, but many others failed to recover economic solvency. Later, during the Tenpō era (1830–1844) a number of *han* leaders instituted further reforms. Notable successes were achieved by Zusho Hiromichi in Satsuma *han*, Tokugawa Nariaki in Mito *han*, and Murata Seifu in Nagato *han* (Chōshū), enabling their *han* to acquire sufficient economic and, subsequently, military strength to become the dominant forces in the Meiji Restoration. They succeeded where the *bakufu* reforms under Mizuno failed: the feudal system in these *han* had not yet degenerated far enough to thwart the implementation of the reform programs.

4. Warrior Impoverishment and the Rise of the Merchants

Where reform programs failed, feudal leaders were obliged finally to borrow extensively from wealthy merchants. *Daimyō* borrowed from their financial agents in the large market cities (*kakeya* and *kuramoto*) or from licensed merchants (mostly money changers) who catered specifically to their wants. When *daimyō* were unable to repay loans they obtained from such financiers, they often refused outright to honor their debts. Such refusals, known as *okotowari*, provoked their creditors to establish "leagues of no lending" (*shimegashi*) as a countermeasure. The *daimyō* were obliged in most cases to yield to the demands of these leagues and to apologize for their arbitrary refusal to repay debts. Ultimately, both the *bakufu* and the *daimyō* granted special privileges to merchants who agreed to lend them money. Such merchants might obtain the right to be treated as *samurai*, and they often received stipends and allowances as *samurai* retainers did. This development represented a reversal of the phenomenon whereby *samurai* were obliged to become merchants and signaled the victory of monetary capital over the feudal order. Thus, as Gamō Kumpei phrased it, "Should one of the great Osaka merchants become angry, all *daimyō* tremble in fear."

Merchants thus achieved a position of economic dominance over the warrior class, but neither mercantile nor moneylending capital was sufficiently powerful to destroy the feudal system. Indeed, the merchants themselves were dependent on the feudal economy for their well-being and may have recognized that destroying it would insure their own ruin. They therefore worked to stave off the system's collapse by cooperating with it. They lent their capital to the *daimyō* and *hatamoto*, invested in reclamation of new fields registered in their own names, and financed the development of the Hokkaido (*Ezo*) fishing industry. They also provided financial assistance for the development of a new form of production—manual labor in factories. Seen from a broader viewpoint, however, commercial and financial capital were not at odds with feudal power, and there was no conspicuous transformation from commercial capital to industrial capital. Industrial capital developed slowly because of the feudal restrictions obstructing its growth.

5. The Division of the Peasant Class

During the first half of the Edo era, most villagers were *honbyakushō* cultivating two or three *chō* of land. In the last half of the era, however, they became differentiated into rich farmers (or big landowners) and poor farmers (or tenant farmers). This process of differentiation had already begun during the Middle Ages, but it was accelerated and became more pronounced after 1700.

Two factors were largely responsible for the emergence of rich landowners (*gōnō*) as a distinct subgroup. First, the availability of new lands for cultivation enabled those with the necessary capital to become large-scale landowners. For example, merchants who developed new fields registered in their names (*chōnin ukeoi shinden*) became large-scale absentee landlords. Those who actually did the work to reclaim these lands became tenant farmers, whose tenancy rights were usually held in perpetuity and were thus very strong. Indeed, these absentee landlords enjoyed little control over their tenants other than exercising the right to collect rent from them.

Scholars are still divided as to whether this investment in the cultivation of new fields may properly be regarded as a manifestation of capitalism. Second, the poverty of peasants bearing very heavy tax burdens and confronted by periodic natural disasters increasingly obliged them to sell their lands to other landowners or merchants, or to mortgage their lands for funds to survive bad years. Once in debt, they found it difficult to repay loans and the interest which accrued, and in many cases they were obliged to forfeit the land to their creditors. Hence, a number of rural landowners and merchants were able to become large-scale landholders by acquiring the land of other farmers.

Despite the emergence of a wealthy class of landowners, the great majority of peasants became poorer during the latter part of the Edo era. Those who lost all of their land were reduced to tenancy on the fields of one or another rich landowner. Many others owned only a few *tan* of cultivated land and could not support themselves without also working as tenants in the fields of bigger landowners. Rents of 50 percent or more of the harvest were paid by tenants to their landlords. In some remote areas, a system akin to slavery existed whereby the rent was paid in labor.

As the money and commodity economy penetrated the countryside, wealthy landowner-farmers not only acquired new land but also began engaging in small-scale industries such as *saké* brewing, soy sauce production, oil rendering, and dyeing, or in commercial enterprises such as dealing in *saké* or oil and pawnshops. As their involvement in these enterprises grew, many ceased laboring on the land and had tenants cultivate their fields. By the end of the Edo era, therefore, two distinct peasant classes had emerged: the wealthy landowner-entrepreneur who no longer worked in the fields, and the tenant farmer (*kosakunin*). These developments meant that the village could no longer function as the economic foundation of the feudal system.

6. Penal Law

The *Kujikata Osadamegaki* was drawn up in 1742, when Yoshimune was seeking to mitigate or abolish the cruel punishments characteristic of the preceding era. While bone-sawing, crucifixion, burning alive, and all other earlier forms of punishment were retained in the *Osadamegaki*, and indeed survived until the

Meiji Restoration, they were applied with much less frequency in the last half of the Edo era. The concept of *enza* still existed, but was invoked far less frequently; *renza* involvement in crimes was punished only mildly.

Generally speaking, the punishments meted out for specific crimes were less severe after Yoshimune's time. The old idea of criminal punishment as a general warning to the public at large (*migorashi*) did not altogether disappear, but alongside it there arose the concept of preventing individual criminals from repeating their misdeeds by reforming them. This development occurred in two stages. The first was the evolution of a system designed to encourage repentance and reform. For example, except in cases of certain very serious crimes, a kind of statute of limitations was applied. If the offender had committed only one crime and thereafter was free from criminal involvement, and more than twelve months had passed before the crime came to light, it was classified as an "evil of the past" (*kyūaku*) and could not be punished. Moreover, the practice of pardoning criminals became widespread. The concept of *kyūaku* absolution was predicated on the individual criminal's repentance and the belief that he would not again break the law, while the pardon system was designed to encourage penitence in order to turn the criminal back to good behavior. The second stage involved penal institutions designed not only to encourage penitence but also to rehabilitate the criminal. In 1790, for example, Matsudaira Sadanobu established a "labor rehabilitation center" (*ninsoku yoseba*) at Tsukudajima in Edo. Persons without a legal residence (*mushukumono*, most of whom had lost their registration as a criminal punishment) were interned there, and later convicts were sent there as well. The intention was to persuade them to renounce a life of crime and provide them with the vocational training required to pursue a fruitful life in some trade. The center was known as an institution of "public education," and the thinking underlying its establishment had more in common with modern liberalistic penal theory than with the draconian ideas behind earlier penal practices.

CHAPTER 5

MONARCHICAL CONSTITUTIONALISM

Kindai, or Modern Period, 1858–1945

The archaic period (*Jōdai*) was characterized by law of uniquely Japanese origins, while the ancient period (*Jōsei*), medieval period (*Chūsei*), and early modern period (*Kinsei*) were marked by the influence of Chinese law in Japan. In contrast, the modern period (*Kindai*) may be classified as a time when European law was introduced into Japan.

Japanese law as formulated under Chinese influence served primarily as an educational and policing instrument, while the European law introduced into Japan during the latter half of the nineteenth century was rooted in the concept of individual rights. Incipient development of the concept of legal rights was apparent in Japan, especially during the Kamakura era, but that development was cut off at the outset by the idea of law as emanating from superior authority, and of lawsuits as requests for favorable judgment from the ruling authority. The notion of popular participation in the formulation of laws was totally alien to Japanese life and thought. Thus, while the influence of European legal thought and practice varied according to time and circumstance, the reordering of the legal system to embrace recognition of individual rights represented an enormous change in orientation and direction.

For the sake of convenience, it is possible to divide the period in which European law influenced Japanese law into three phases:

The beginning phase (1858–1881). The *baku-han* (*bakufu* and *han*) system of law survived until 1869, after which Japanese law was subjected to a variety of old and new influences. The laws of the new Meiji government were greatly influenced by European legal theory, particularly by the French liberal doctrine of popular rights. Indeed, the government carried out a number of reforms on the basis of these theories. However, the Meiji leadership was also deeply influenced by the idea of restoring the ancient system of imperial rule in Japan, and was therefore inclined to resurrect older legal practices—not feudal law, but the *ritusryō* antecedents and the sinified legal system they spawned. The influence of these old Japanese laws was reflected in the Meiji government's Essence of the New Criminal Code (*Shinritsu Kōryō*, 1870) and Amended Criminal Code and Statutes (*Kaitei Ritsurei*, 1873). The diverse ideas interacting in the formulation of laws during the 1858–1881 period clearly mark these years as a time of transition from the early modern to the modern period.

The middle phase (1881–1931): The implementation under French legal influence of the Penal Code (*Kei Hō*) and the Code of Criminal Procedure (*Chizai Hō*) in 1882 marked an epoch in Japanese legal history. Law in the ancient style disappeared to be replaced entirely by modern codes, particularly by penal law based on the assumption that crimes and punishments must be limited by the scope of explicit legal enactment. This approach to penal law, in conjunction with the imperial rescript of 1881 promising the establishment of a parliament by 1890, symbolized Japan's maturation as a modern nation-state. Important legal developments then followed in rapid succession. The Meiji Constitution was issued in 1889, and the Imperial Diet convened for the first time in 1890. Further, in order to win Western respect for Japan's legal institutions and obtain revision of the unequal treaties concluded with Western countries in the 1850s, Japanese leaders drew up an extensive body of judicial codes, making the country a nation governed by law. A Code of Criminal Procedure, Code of Civil Procedure, Civil Code, and Commercial Code were rapidly promulgated, and in 1899 commercial treaties placing Japan on an equal footing with other signatory nations were concluded with the Western powers. German law had by now replaced French legal theory and practice as the dominant European influence on Japanese law, and in many other respects as well Japan seemed to have come very far indeed from the 1858–1881 period.

From 1890 to around 1931, the Meiji Constitution was observed; its provisions upheld the freedom to enter into contracts, the inviolability of private property rights, and the principle of individual responsibility. This era was characterized by the growth of capitalism and the spread of democratic ideas, especially after World War I; these ideas culminated in 1925 with the enactment of the universal male suffrage act.

The final phase (1931–1945): At the same time, however, the Japanese economy was embroiled in the worldwide depression, and in 1931 the Japanese military provoked the well-known Manchurian Incident, a military engagement of Japanese and Chinese troops that began with a bomb explosion on the South Manchurian Railway in the vicinity of Mukden. From 1931 to 1945, the nation experienced a prolonged "period of emergency" (*hijō-ji*) marked by growing militarism and reactionary political thought and behavior. Emphasis on national defense developed into political dictatorship, which repressed individual rights on the one hand and controlled the economy on the other. Even during this unhappy era, some social legislation was enacted, but its purpose was invariably to enhance the country's military strength. The principle of parliamentary government was steadily eroded. Symptomatic of these developments were the enactment of the National General Mobilization Act in 1938 and the absorption of the struggling political parties into the Imperial Rule Assistance Association (*Taisei Yokusan Kai*) in 1940. Finally, in December 1941, Japan launched the Pacific War, which lasted until August 1945. In short, the period from 1931 to 1945 saw the degeneration of the functions of the Meiji Constitution and the end of the modern period.

A. The Collapse of Feudalism and the Modern *Dajōkan* System
Beginning Phase, 1858–1881

1. Collapse of Bakufu Feudalism and Imperial Restoration

During the last years of the Edo era there were several occasions when the *bakufu*, on its own initiative or in response to a request from the imperial court, conveyed its opinion on domestic or diplomatic affairs to the throne. At no time, however, had the *bakufu* specifically sought imperial sanction for any political decision taken by the Edo authorities. This imperious *bakufu* attitude toward the court changed when Commodore Perry of the United States appeared in Japanese waters in 1853 and demanded that Japan open its doors to foreign intercourse and enter into trade relations with other countries. Perry's demand was made in the face of a traditional *bakufu* policy of national isolation (*sakoku*) which had closed Japan off from virtually all contact with the outside world since the early part of the seventeenth century. Despite the enormous importance attached to the *sakoku* policy by all domestic political forces in Japan, the presence of the American gunboats left the *bakufu* with no alternative to signing a treaty of friendship with the United States in 1854. Three years later, the *bakufu* was obliged to sign another treaty of amity and commerce with the American consul-general, Townsend Harris.

These treaties marked the abandonment of the traditional *sakoku* policy, and the *bakufu* was extremely apprehensive about their effect on domestic political opinion and the views of the court. To dilute its responsibility, the *bakufu* sought imperial sanction for the commercial treaty negotiated with Harris, but the court denied permission by imperial edict. There were two important consequences of this refusal. First, the *bakufu* was obliged to ratify the commercial treaty on its own responsibility in 1858. Equally important, however, its prestige had been severely impaired by conflict with the court. This humiliating blow made it difficult for the *bakufu* to enlist active cooperation and advice from the other *daimyō* on how best to deal with foreign pressures. In short, the *bakufu*'s approach to marshaling support at court and among the *daimyō* for its foreign policy led these forces to doubt the efficacy of the *shōgun*'s government and to question its right to monopolize national political power. The *bakufu*'s foreign and domestic policies at this juncture touched off a series of developments which culminated in the downfall of the whole system, and the year 1858 is consequently regarded by many historians as the starting point of the modern period.

After 1858, *bakufu* power vis-à-vis the court and several of the powerful *tozama daimyō* steadily eroded. For the first time, the more powerful *daimyō* established direct contacts with the court, and the court itself began to engage in political activities. Within a few years, the *bakufu*'s right to monopolize national political power had been called into open question. Chōshū (Nagato *han*), one of the most powerful of the *tozama* domains, led those who called for the overthrow of the *bakufu*. Satsuma *han*, another powerful *tozama* domain, took a less extreme position and worked for a new alignment of national power in which authority would be shared by the *bakufu*, the court, and the most prominent *tozama* domains—the so-called *kōbu-gattai* compromise formula. After the *bakufu* launched two military expeditions against the rebellious Chōshū forces in 1864 and 1866, however, Chōshū and Satsuma agreed to work jointly for the restoration of imperial rule in place of the *bakufu*, and enlisted the support of several influential court nobles.

It was precisely at this juncture, in 1866, that *shōgun* Tokugawa Iemochi died. Tokugawa Keiki (Yoshinobu) succeeded him as head of the Tokugawa house but declined initially to assume the position of *shōgun*. This decision was based on the view that while the position of chief of the warrior houses (*buke no tōryō*) rightly belonged to the current head of the Tokugawa house and carried with it the prerogatives of political authority, it was distinct from the position of *sei-i-tai-shōgun*. It was commonly recognized that the *shōgun* historically was responsible for attacking and defeating foreign barbarians, and Keiki, recognizing the impossibility of driving the Western powers off, was reluctant to assume the difficult position which would confront the holder of this post.

This assessment of the situation did not, however, prevent Keiki's supporters from insisting that he accept the position of *shōgun*, and at the end of 1866 he was finally obliged to do so. Within a month, Emperor Kōmei—one of the last important advocates of the *kōbu-gattai* compromise approach to resolving the domestic political turmoil—died, anti-*bakufu* activity in Satsuma and Chōshū intensified, and the *bakufu*'s position became even more tenuous. Even at this critical moment, however, Keiki attempted to reform *bakufu* administration. With the support of French ambassador Léon Roches, he abolished the older system of "monthly attendance" (*sankin-kotai*) and appointed his *rōjū* to serve as chief officers or ministers (*sōsai*) for the army, navy, internal affairs, finance, and foreign affairs. This new structure, established in 1867, approximated a type of cabinet system. Moreover, Keiki was finally able to persuade the court to sanction the *bakufu* decision to open the port of Hyōgo to foreign trade.

During 1867, two influential court nobles, Iwakura Tomomi and Sanjō Sanetomi, continued to agitate for an imperial restoration. Chōshū and Satsuma also pressed ahead with their plans to overthrow the *bakufu*, and were now joined by the Aki *han*. As matters came to a head on November 9, Satsuma and Chōshū were able to enlist Iwakura's assistance in obtaining a secret imperial order to overthrow the *bakufu*. Forces more sympathetic to Keiki and the *bakufu*, however, were also active. Gotō Shōjirō, a prominent political leader in Tosa *han*, had argued that the *shōgun* might retain an influential position in any *kōbu-gattai* style of political structure, and Gotō's viewpoint was now embraced by the former *daimyō* of Tosa, Yamanouchi Yōdō (Toyoshige). Warned of the plans Satsuma and Chōshū were then preparing, and having close relationships with the *bakufu*, Yamanouchi had Gotō submit his plan directly to the *bakufu* with his endorsement. Keiki read Gotō's memorial and approved its contents. On November 9, the same day Satsuma and Chōshū obtained imperial permission to attack Keiki's forces, the *shōgun* informed the court of his desire to return political power to the emperor. However, the political power Keiki proposed to return referred only to the right to govern the *daimyō* and did not affect his control over *bakufu* domains (which amounted to seven million *koku*). The court therefore sought to persuade Keiki to "contribute" two million *koku* to the emperor, but the outbreak of war soon interrupted negotiations, Keiki was declared an enemy of the court, and the *bakufu* domains were confiscated. The rights of the *daimyō*, meanwhile, remained intact, and the emperor succeeded to the position of "chief of the warriors" (*buke no toryō*). The role of the emperor as a feudal sovereign was ended in the formal sense by the return of *han* subjects and lands to him in 1869, but continued in fact until 1871, when the *han* were abolished completely.

2. Restoration of Imperial Rule (Ōsei Fukko)

On the day after Keiki agreed to restore political power to the emperor, the court approved his petition, and the imperial restoration became an accomplished fact. On January 3, 1868, a formal declaration of restoration was issued and a new administrative structure was established in conformity with the ancient style of direct imperial control over political affairs. The posts of *sesshō*, *kanpaku*, and *sei-i-tai-shōgun*, whose holders had stood for so long between the emperor and actual political power, were abolished. In their place three new posts were established directly under the emperor: *sōsai* (prime minister), *gijō* (senior councilors), and *san'yo* (junior councilors). Imperial Prince Arisugawa Taruhito was designated *sōsai* while the remaining posts were allotted to other princes, courtiers, *daimyō*, and *samurai* who had worked for the imperial cause.

It was also on January 3 that supporters of the restoration made important decisions about the role of the Tokugawa family in the new regime. While Keiki and his troops waited in Osaka, a conference of restoration leaders was held at the Kogosho (Small Imperial Palace) in Kyoto to debate the composition of the new imperial government. Although Yamanouchi Yōdō and others argued that the new state should be modeled along the lines proposed in Gotō Shōjirō's earlier memorial, and should thus include Keiki and *bakufu* forces, Iwakura joined with the Satsuma and Chōshū representatives in overruling this view, insisting that the *bakufu* be destroyed and Keiki relinquish his position.

When the *bakufu* retainers and the *samurai* of Aizu, Kuwano, and other *han* backing Keiki learned of Iwakura's success at the Kogosho conference, they were enraged and swore to resist the imperial forces. However, they were soon defeated in battles at Toba and Fushimi (near Kyoto), and Arisugawa led the imperial forces toward Edo in pursuit of the ex-*shōgun* and his backers. When Keiki reached his castle in Edo, he decided to submit to imperial authority, and through the mediating efforts of his advisor Katsu Kaishū (Yasuyoshi), Edo Castle was surrendered without bloodshed. Keiki was then confined to his residence in Mito and yielded leadership of the Tokugawa house to Tayasu Kamenosuke (thenceforth known as Tokugawa Iesato). All of the Tokugawa domains were confiscated, although Iesato was later granted a fief of 700,000 *koku* in the area of Suruga and Tōtōmi provinces. Resistance by *bakufu* supporters continued only sporadically thereafter. One band of *bakufu* loyalists, the *Shōgitai*, offered resistance in the Ueno section of Edo, and a federation of *daimyō* in northern Honshu, led by the *daimyō* of Aizu *han*, Matsudaira Katamori, held out against the imperial forces until October 1868. The last bastion of resistance, a force led by *bakufu* retainer Enomoto Buyō (Takeaki), surrendered at Hakodate in Hokkaido in June 1869.

Meanwhile, the new government had already begun its administration. On April 6, 1868, the emperor issued a most important five-article Charter Oath (*Gokajō no Goseimon*), outlining the principles to be followed by his government :

1. Deliberative assemblies shall be established on an extensive scale and all measures shall be determined by public discussion.

2. High and low shall unite in carrying out the nation's plans with vigor.

3. All classes shall be allowed to fulfill their just aspirations and be content.

4. Base customs of the past shall be discontinued, and just and equitable principles of nature shall become the basis of our policy.

5. Knowledge shall be sought throughout the world in order that the welfare of the empire may be promoted.

While the first article was of course not intended as a declaration of modern democracy, the Charter Oath was nevertheless remarkably progressive for its time. It affirmed the new political principles of heeding public opinion and opening the country to cordial relations with the rest of the world.

In June the new government adopted a new fundamental law called the *Seitaisho*. A mixture of American and ancient Japanese concepts of public administration, the *Seitaisho* reestablished the Nara era *dajōkan* (grand council of state) as the locus of supreme political power under the emperor.* Following the American concept of a tripartite division of governmental powers, *dajōkan* authority was divided among the *giseikan* (legislative assembly), *keihōkan* (judiciary), and *gyōseikan* (executive administration). The administrative affairs of the *gyōseikan* were further divided among the departments of religious affairs, finance, military affairs, and foreign affairs. The *giseikan* was subdivided into upper and lower

* While the grand council was called the *daijōkan* in the Nara era and *dajōkan* in the Meiji era, they are written in Japanese with the same characters.

chambers. The lower chamber served in an advisory capacity to the upper, and was made up of *samurai* delegates from the various *han*. This body changed form several times and was named, in turn, *Kōshi taisakusho, Kōgisho*, and finally *Shūgiin*. The *Seitaisho* also provided for the election of higher officials by officeholders, but only one such election was ever held.

These administrative reforms were accompanied by other departures from tradition. The new government took note of the fact that Edo was the political center of the nation and, in September 1868, formally renamed it Tokyo ("eastern capital"). In November, the emperor moved in formal procession from Kyoto to the new imperial capital and took up permanent residence there in the beginning of 1869.

In general, the new regime placed heavy emphasis on the importance of the emperor in ruling the nation. Following the death of Emperor Kōmei in 1866, his fourteen-year-old son Mutsuhito succeeded him, and it was in his name that all official pronouncements of the new government were made. In October 1868, the emperor announced that the commemorative name (*nengō*) for the years of his reign would be "Meiji" ("enlightened rule") and that henceforth, each emperor would designate only one *nengō* during his reign.* The imperial restoration of 1867–1868 is thus known as the Meiji Restoration, and the years from 1868 to 1912, when Mutsuhito died, are known as the Meiji era.

3. Centralization: The Significance of Hanseki Hōkan and Haihan Chiken

Keiki's return of political power to the imperial institution in November 1867 did not affect his control over *bakufu* territory; nor did it affect the relatively autonomous status of the *daimyō* within their own domains. As stated earlier, his action did little more than perpetuate the feudal system, with the emperor replacing the *shōgun* as chief of the warrior houses. The new Meiji government, however, quickly agreed that Japan must be modernized along lines followed by the advanced countries of the West, and they further believed that a vital prerequisite to modernization was the replacement of the decentralized system of *daimyō* rule with an

---

* Emperor Kōmei ruled from 1847 to 1867, during which time there had been six *nengō: Kaei, Ansei, Man'en, Bunkyū, Genji,* and *Keiō*.

integrated and centralized system of local administration. The government's first steps toward centralization were taken shortly after the collapse of military resistance to the restoration. Lands of the defeated *bakufu* and *daimyō* opposing the imperial cause were confiscated and reorganized as administrative units or prefectures under the central government (*fu* and *ken*).

These measures were not applied to neutral *daimyō* nor to those who had supported the restoration. The feudal system thus continued in force under imperial leadership, and *han*, *fu*, and *ken* served as the basic units of local government. The new government, dominated by representatives of Satsuma, Chōshū, Tosa, and Hizen *han*, sought to promote further centralization by persuading the *daimyō* of these four *han* to restore to the imperial government political authority over their lands and subjects. In March 1869, the four *daimyō* jointly petitioned the throne to accept their "return of enfeoffed land and subjects" (*hanseki hōkan*), and other *daimyō* soon followed their example. The court granted this petition in July, and ordered other *daimyō* who had yet to make similar offers to surrender their fiefs. Once all *daimyō* had complied with this policy, the government immediately appointed them to serve as governors of their respective *han*. However, this policy involved much more than a simple change in nomenclature; *daimyō* who had previously been semi-autonomous local rulers in their domains now became officials of the central government, serving at the emperor's pleasure.

The *hanseki hōkan* program ended the existence of the feudal political structure in form, but as yet it had little effect on political relations within each *han*. To integrate local areas more completely into the central administrative structure, the government now sought to abolish the *han* completely and establish prefectures (*ken*) in their stead. Anticipating the possibility of armed resistance, the government organized an imperial guard (*goshinpei*) comprised of troops from Satsuma, Chōshū, and Tosa before proceeding with its plans. However, many of the ex-*daimyō* governors no longer wished to bear the financial responsibility for governing their domains and actively encouraged the government to abolish their *han*. Consequently, the government was able to abolish the *han* and create prefectures (*haihan chiken*) in August 1871 without encountering any military challenge to its orders.

The ex-*daimyō* governors were all recalled to Tokyo and replaced by new governors (*fu-chiji* and *ken-rei*, or, later, *ken-chiji*), many of whom hailed from Satsuma and Chōshū. At the same time, the number of administrative units was greatly consolidated, from over 260 *han* to 72 *ken* and 3 *fu* (prefectural units of special importance—Tokyo, Osaka, and Kyoto). Further consolidation took place in 1889 when the number of *ken* was reduced to forty-three.

4. The Modernized Dajōkan System

As the government's program of regional integration proceeded, it inevitably became necessary to devise a new structure of central administration as well. Discarding the tripartite division of powers contained in the *Seitaisho*, the Meiji regime was motivated by its own restorationist ideology to restore the eighth-century political structure established by the Taihō Code. A new civil service code (*Shokuin Rei*) was issued in 1869, and to the original Meiji *dajōkan* was added a *jingikan* (ministry of *Shintō* affairs). The top *dajōkan* posts were a minister of the left (*sadaijin*), a minister of the right (*udaijin*), three (later four) vice-ministers (*dainagon*), and several councilors (*sangi*). They presided over the work of six ministries: civil affairs, finance, military affairs, foreign affairs, justice, and imperial household. A ministry of industrial affairs was added the following year.

As the process of centralization accelerated with the abolition of the *han* and the establishment of the prefectural system, the government made further adjustments in the central administrative structure. In September 1871, the *dajōkan* was again divided into three departments, the main department (*sei-in*), left department (*sa-in*), and right department (*u-in*). The *sei-in* was the office through which the emperor was to exercise personal control over the affairs of state; it was the focal point of the politics of the time. Its chief officials were the *dajōdaijin* (prime minister), *nagon* (ministers, later specified as minister of the left [*sadaijin*], and minister of the right [*udaijin*]) and *sangi*. The *sa-in* was an assembly of officials who made legislative recommendations to the *sei-in*, while the *u-in* was essentially a conference of ministers and vice-ministers from each ministry, meeting to discuss administrative problems and policies.

The *sei-in* was thus the nucleus of the structure. Up to this point, the government had emphasized the importance of direct imperial rule, largely as a means to foster concentration of power in the central government. Once political power had in fact been centralized with the abolition of the *han*, the emphasis on direct imperial rule faded from view. Conversely, the successful effort by government leaders to centralize political power now began to evoke complaints from outside the government that the Meiji regime had become a system of bureaucratic absolutism. This charge was to be repeated frequently during ensuing years, particularly as officials in the bureaucracy increasingly regarded themselves as the emperor's administrators rather than as servants of the people.

The *dajōkan* was restructured again in 1873 in order to further concentrate power in the *sei-in*. While its chief officers, the prime minister and ministers of the left and right, were established as directly responsible for "assisting" the emperor in governing, the *sangi* now became a type of cabinet which decided all important governmental questions collegially. This shift in the locus of real political power reflected the fact that most of the courtiers and *daimyō* who had held top positions in the Meiji government at its inception were by now eased out of the government. Real power passed to lower-ranking *samurai* from Satsuma, Chōshū, Hizen, and Tosa, who held *sangi* posts. Of the original group of court nobles in the government, only Iwakura Tomomi and Sanjō Sanetomi retained influence after this period.

The first important division of opinion among the lower *samurai* now moving into prominence in the government concerned the setting of official priorities at home and abroad. In 1871, Iwakura, Ōkubo Toshimichi (of Satsuma) and Kido Takayoshi (commonly Kōin) (of Chōshū) led a delegation to Europe and the United States in the hope that the Western nations would be willing to renegotiate the unequal treaties they had signed with Japan in the 1850s. The mission failed, but Iwakura, Ōkubo, and Kido returned from abroad persuaded that Japan should seek international equality by concentrating all its energies on internal reform and national self-strengthening. They returned to Japan in 1873 to find that in their absence, Saigō Takamori (of Satsuma) and other members of the caretaker government had decided to send an expeditionary force to Korea. Iwakura, Ōkubo, and Kido opposed this foreign adventure vehemently, asserting that Japan must first place its own house in order before expanding abroad. They were ultimately able to cancel the government's decision to invade Korea, but the reversal provoked supporters of the invasion to resign from their *sangi* positions. Ōkubo and Kido thereafter became the central figures in the government, but Kido resigned within a short time in protest against Ōkubo's willingness to placate the advocates of expansion with a small punitive expedition to Taiwan. Ōkubo now stood alone as the key government leader, a situation which prompted his enemies to denounce the government, declaring it to be run by *han* cliques, with no reflection of the people's wishes as the Charter Oath had promised.

Ōkubo responded to these criticisms by meeting with Kido in 1875 (at the so-called Osaka Conference). By making policy concessions, he persuaded Kido to return to the government as a *sangi*. As a result of their agreement, the *dajōkan* was again radically reformed before the year was out. The *sa-in* and *u-in* were abolished, and a senate (*genrōin*) was created to broaden participation in legislative activities in accordance with an expanded interpretation of the intent of the Charter Oath. Meetings of local officials were convened to probe popular sentiment and to help delineate the national interest, with an eye to moving gradually toward the establishment of a constitutional system. A supreme court (*daishin'in*) was also created independent of other official institutions, in order to strengthen the judiciary. It is possible to discern in these reforms an inclination to establish a tripartite division of powers among the executive, the legislature, and the judiciary, but the changes effected at this time were of a severely limited nature. The *genrōin*, for example, was made up not of popularly elected representatives but of appointed government officials. Likewise the meetings held locally to ascertain popular feeling were not public assemblies but mere conferences of local officials. Nevertheless, this was the most progressive *dajōkan* system ever to be devised, and it is appropriate therefore to designate it as a "modernized *dajōkan*."

While the government under Ōkubo's leadership was able to regain Kido's backing, its domestic policies precluded any reconciliation with Saigō and many others who had left the government in 1873. Indeed, in the same year, almost immediately after

Saigō's resignation, the government issued a conscription act, ordering all male subjects to serve a fixed number of years on active or reserve duty in a new national army. Three years later, ex-*samurai* were prohibited from exercising their former privilege of carrying swords; with this move, the government effectively disarmed all citizens outside the armed forces. These measures fanned the discontent of many former *samurai*, who felt that they had been unjustly deprived of their privileged status. A number of ex-*samurai* rebellions occurred during the early 1870s, culminating in the large-scale Satsuma Rebellion under Saigō Takamori's leadership in 1877. The new conscript army of commoners demonstrated, however, that it was superior to Saigō's ex-*samurai* forces; Saigō was obliged to concede defeat and took his own life. The demonstrated effectiveness of the new army in maintaining domestic order precluded any further outbreaks of rebellious *samurai*, and the dissolution of *han* and establishment of prefectures proceeded.

At the moment of their greatest triumph, however, death also claimed Kido (in 1877, from illness) and Ōkubo (in 1878, at the hand of an assassin). In the void left by their passing, Iwakura, Ōkuma Shigenobu (of Hizen), and Itō Hirobumi (of Chōshū) became the most powerful men in the Meiji government.

5. The Idea of Government in accord with Public Opinion (Kōgi Yoron)

The concept of governing in accord with public opinion permeated Japanese politics slowly, and acquired new meanings as time passed. The first effort by any Japanese government to solicit "public opinion" in connection with policy-making was made by the *bakufu* in 1853 and was limited to seeking the views of the *daimyō* on how to deal with the demands of Commodore Perry. Even this small step, however, broke a tradition of *bakufu* absolutism that had been maintained for over two centuries, and it opened the way for increasingly frequent consultation by the *bakufu* with the *daimyō* on important issues of state.

Interest in relating public opinion to political decision-making was greatly stimulated as well by growing knowledge and curiosity about Western systems of parliamentary government. Japanese were aware of the existence and nature of parliamentary government as early as the 1820s, and interest grew rapidly during the last years of *bakufu* rule when foreign ideas began to penetrate the country. During the mid-1850s Hashimoto Sanai of Echizen *han* wrote treatises on Western parliamentary systems and Yokoi Shōnan of Kumamoto *han* advocated the establishment of a parliament of *daimyō*. Early in the 1860s Yokoi's idea received the endorsement of two *bakufu* officials, Ōkubo Tadahiro and Katsu Kaishū, and a Japanese delegation sent to the United States in 1860 visited the American Congress in session. Nishi Amane, an advisor to Tokugawa Keiki, brought a proposal for a *daimyō* parliament to the *shōgun's* attention in 1867, so it is reasonable to conclude that Keiki himself had at least a rudimentary understanding of parliamentary forms. It has been argued, in fact, that when he offered to return the prerogatives of the *shōgun* to the throne in November 1867, Keiki intended to assume the influential position of president of an imperially sanctioned parliament of *daimyō*. If, indeed, he ever entertained such hopes, they were effectively stymied by Iwakura and his supporters at the Kogosho Conference on January 3, 1868.

The notion of linking government decisions to public discussion appeared again in the Charter Oath of the new Meiji government. In early drafts of the proclamation, the article indicating that "deliberative assemblies of lords (*rekkō*) shall be established . . . and all measures shall be determined in accord with public discussion" specified that a *daimyō* parliament should provide the institutional setting for soliciting public opinion. Some historians therefore insist that the mention of "deliberative assemblies" was a specific reference to the proposed *daimyō* parliament. However, . since the draftsmen consciously deleted all mention of a parliament limited to *daimyō*, it seems more appropriate to believe that "public discussion" was to be open to participation by the general public as well as by *daimyō*. Indeed, the *Seitaisho* adopted in June 1868 did not mention a *daimyō* parliament but did establish a bicameral *giseikan* in which imperial princes, nobles, *daimyō*, *samurai*, and even commoners might serve as members of the upper chamber while *han* representatives (*kōshi*) selected by the *daimyō* served in the lower. Although the *giseikan* was not a popularly elected body, it provided the opportunity for debate and solicitation of "public opinion."

The Meiji government's respect for public opinion proved to be

short-lived, however. As it became more confident of its own stability, the government became more autocratic and increasingly
unreceptive to popular sentiment. The fate of the legislative branch
of government reflected this trend. The lower section of the *giseikan*
was renamed *kōshi taisakusho* and *kōgisho* later in 1868, and *shūgiin*
in 1869, but it was never powerful under any name. In the reforms
of 1871, the *sa-in* was established as an assembly elected by vote
of government officials, and in 1873 the *shūgiin* was abolished as
redundant. Two years later the *sa-in* was replaced by the *genrōin*.

In response to the government's evisceration of early representative institutions and its growing absolutism, a number of discon-
tented ex-*samurai* began a movement for a parliament of publicly
elected representatives. The philosophical underpinning of the
movement was provided by the writings of John Stuart Mill, Her-
bert Spencer, and Adam Smith, as well as by Jean-Jacques Rousseau's theory of natural rights. Utilitarian ideas spread through
Nakamura Masanao's translations of Samuel Smiles's *Self-Help*
(in Japanese, *Saigoku Risshihen*) and Mill's *On Liberty* (*Jiyū no Ri*)
in 1871 as well as through Fukuzawa Yukichi's early Meiji classic,
Gakumon no Susume. The principal proponents of Rousseau's ideas
were Nakae Chōmin (who translated Rousseau's *Du contrat social*
as *Min'yaku Yakkai* in 1882) and Ōi Kentarō.

6. The Popular Rights Movement (Jiyū Minken Undō)

Increasingly neglecting the principle of government by public
discussion which it had at first championed, the Meiji government
grew more and more despotic, particularly after the debate over
the Korean expedition and the consequent resignations of *sangi*
from Hizen and Tosa. The government appeared as a Satsuma-
Chōshū dominated clique, and protests against "bureaucratic
despotism" became ever stronger; at the same time, political
theories such as Rousseau's doctrine of natural rights were being
introduced into Japan. The men who had just left the government
after losing the dispute over Korea were able to take advantage of
these trends, and in January 1874, Itagaki Taisuke (of Tosa), Gotō
Shōjirō (Tosa), Soejima Taneomi (Hizen) and Etō Shinpei (Hizen)
presented the government with a memorial recommending the
establishment of a popularly elected assembly. Although based on
the theory of natural rights, the memorial was strongly statist in

tone; it failed, moreover, to demand the right of suffrage for all citizens, limiting it instead to the former *samurai* plus the wealthier peasants and merchants. Itagaki and his colleagues formed a political association (*Aikoku Kōtō*) to promote their objectives, but the organization quickly disintegrated when Etō returned to Hizen to lead a short-lived *samurai* rebellion against the government in 1874. Itagaki returned to Tosa to organize a new society, the *Risshisha*, with Kataoka Kenkichi and other advocates of the ideals of liberty and popular rights. In 1875, the society expanded into a nationwide body with headquarters in Osaka and was renamed *Aikokusha* (Patriotic Society). The Aikokusha served as a national federation of groups seeking to promote liberty and popular rights.

The founding of the *Aikokusha*, in January 1875, prompted the government to appease the opposition by reforms like the above-mentioned modernization of the *dajōkan* and, in 1879, the opening of prefectural assemblies. Compromise, however, was accompanied by a number of measures intended to repress the popular rights movement. Notably, the government issued the Press Act (*Shinbun Jōrei*) and the Libel Act (*Zanbō Ritsu*) in 1875 to stifle public debate on and criticism of its policies. Nevertheless, the *Aikokusha* reorganized in 1878, and in 1880 changed its name to the League for the Promotion of a Parliament (*Kokkai Kisei Dōmei*); after that year, the name again changed to the Association of Supporters of a Japanese Parliament (*Dai-Nippon Kokkai Kisei Yūshi Kōkai*). Several petition campaigns were organized by popular rights advocates, and demands for a parliament poured into government offices as the movement reached a crescendo in the press and in public forums. The government responded by issuing a law severely restricting public gatherings for political purposes, the Regulations for Public Meetings (*Shūkai Jōrei*, 1880). By this time, many private drafts for a constituion were in circulation, and even within the government, the *genrōin* was working on a proposed constitution (*kokken*). (The draft was rejected in 1880 for not adequately reflecting current national conditions.)

In the midst of these developments, word leaked out, in 1881, that the government-owned property of the Hokkaido Development Office, in which fourteen million yen had been invested, was about to be sold to the Kansai Trading Company organized by

Godai Tomoatsu of Satsuma and Nakano Goichi of Chōshū. When the terms of sale were revealed (380,000 yen, to be paid over thirty years without interest), government leaders were severely criticized for virtually giving away national assets to their cohorts from the same *han*. Embarrassed by this attack on "bureaucratic despotism," the government canceled the sale, dismissed Ōkuma Shigenobu from his office of *sangi* for advocating the immediate convening of a national assembly, and had the emperor issue an edict promising the opening of a parliament by 1890.

These concessions ended the political turmoil for the moment, and the opposition turned its attention to forming political parties in anticipation of the creation of a parliament. Itagaki, Gotō Shō-jirō, Nakae Chōmin, and Nakajima Nobuyuki established the Jiyūtō (Liberal Party) with a platform advocating radical French theories of liberty and popular rights; they won the support of ex-*samurai* and impoverished peasants dissatisfied with the government. Ōkuma, Inukai Tsuyoshi, and Ozaki Yukio formed the Rik-ken Kaishintō (Constitutional Reform Party) with a platform propounding moderate English-style parliamentarianism; they were backed by the intelligentsia and landlord groups. A third party, the Rikken Teiseitō (Imperial Rule Party) was organized by Fukuchi Gen'ichirō and others to serve as a pro-government group, counterbalancing the opposition parties.

7. Revision of the Land Tax and Disposal of Samurai Stipends

From the very beginning, the Meiji government suffered from severe financial problems. Lacking any independent source of income before the *bakufu* and Tokugawa house lands had been secured, the chief financial planner of the government, Yuri Kimi-masa (Mitsuoka Hachirō) managed to obtain funds for government operations in the early post-restoration years only by issuing unbacked *dajōkan* paper currency and extracting contributions (*goyōkin*) from the wealthy merchant houses of Mitsui, Ono, and Shimada. Yuri's policies marked the beginning of a long and close association between the government and "political-merchant" (*seishō*) houses like Mitsui.

While these emergency policies permitted the government to survive temporarily, it was faced with the immediate need to secure revenue and cut expenditures, which meant revising the land tax system on the one hand and gradually phasing out *samurai* stipends on the other. The overwhelmingly dominant source of wealth was agriculture, and land taxes (*chiso*) accordingly occupied first place among sources of government revenue. By 1873, when the Land Tax Reform Ordinance (*Chiso Kaisei Hō*) was promulgated, land taxes amounted to 70 percent of total annual revenue and 80 percent of regular government income. The system of taxation had lacked uniformity, however, due to regional variations that had grown up under the decentralized administration of *daimyō* and *bakufu*. The proceeds obtainable, moreover, were uncertain, as the tax was paid in kind rather than in money. The newly promulgated system sought to modernize the tax and ensure that revenue from it would never fall below a certain level. All land was to be surveyed and assigned a definite money value, and the tax was to be paid by the owner; the responsibility of the village for tax payment was eliminated. A uniform rate of taxation was imposed: at first, 3 percent of assessed value. By 1881, the new system was in full operation.

Despite its apparent impartiality, however, the fixed land tax weighed heavily on poor farmers, since they were required to pay the same amount every year regardless of the size of their harvest. It was far easier for a wealthy landowner or farmer with accumulated wealth to meet his tax obligations in bad years than for impoverished peasants living near subsistence levels. The new tax law thus provoked widespread agrarian discontent, culminating in the well-known peasant uprisings of 1876 in Mie and Ibaraki prefectures. The government finally agreed in 1877 to reduce the tax rate to 2.5 percent.

Inasmuch as the responsibility for making tax payments under the new law shifted from the village as a collective unit to the individual landowner, the government took steps to clarify the concept of land ownership in modern terms. Land certificates (*chiken*) were issued in 1872 as proof of ownership; these could be transferred from someone selling his land to the purchaser. The same type of certificate was issued for cultivated fields, residential land, forest areas, and ponds and marshes, thereby standardizing ownership rights to various types of property. Once the certificates had been issued, there was no longer any possibility that two parties could legitimately claim ownership to the same land. After the implementation of the 1873 tax reform, the certificate system was extended throughout the nation, contributing greatly to the modernization of prevailing concepts of property rights.

A second great problem confronting the financial specialists of the Meiji government was posed by the burden of stipends (*chitsuroku*). Shortly after the restoration of imperial rule, the new regime awarded stipends to a number of courtiers, *daimyō*, and *samurai* in recognition of their services on behalf of the imperial cause. In addition to these stipends (called *shōtenroku*), the government assumed responsibility for the payment of all *daimyō* retainers' stipends when the *daimyō* "returned" their fiefs to the throne and became governors of their *han*. The government's plan was to commute these stipends into lump sum cash payments, but in view of the many problems attending such an approach, it finally issued special bonds in 1876 to those entitled to receive stipends and formally ended the stipend system in 1877. This resolved the problem of stipends, but it left the government with the heavy financial burden of meeting the bond obligations for many years to come.

8. Abolition of the Confucian Status System

The system of social ranks developed under the feudal order was reformed slowly but steadily by the Meiji government. In 1869, a new nobility (*kazoku*) was established to embrace the court nobility and ex-*daimyō*. The *samurai* class was divided into two, with upper *samurai* now designated as *shizoku* and lower *samurai* as *sotsu*. In 1871, degrading status titles were abolished. In 1872, the *sotsu* class was abolished and its upper echelons integrated into the *shizoku* class. The remaining *sotsu* were relegated to *heimin* (commoner) status along with the rest of the population.

In the resulting three-class system consisting of *kazoku*, *shizoku*, and *heimin*, the distance between the various ranks was greatly reduced. After 1871, for example, *kazoku* and *shizoku* were permitted to engage in agriculture, commerce, and industry, as long as they were not serving in the government. In 1872 peasants were granted the freedom to change occupations as well. Men of all ranks were also allowed to change residence without restriction. *Heimin* were permitted in 1870 to adopt surnames for the first time and in 1873 were permitted to bear arms as conscripts in the new national army. Hence, for the first time since Hideyoshi's "sword-hunt," commoners and warriors (*shizoku*) shared the duty of military service. In 1875, all commoners were obliged to adopt surnames.

These social changes affected former *samurai* more than any other group. They had lost both their lords and their occupations, and many of their former privileges were no longer exclusively theirs. Most found themselves in dire economic straits, since the bonds they received from the government were apportioned on the basis of their often small and inadequate feudal incomes. The government also offered them loans to start businesses or engage in cultivating newly opened lands. Some did open small businesses, and while a few like Iwasaki Yatarō and Shibusawa Eiichi succeeded, many failed for lack of experience or capital. Others made their way as policemen, teachers, or minor officials, but many just seethed with anger at the policies of the government. Their discontent erupted into rebellions such as those led by Saigō and Etō, or it was channeled into the popular rights movement.

Despite the hardships suffered by the *samurai* class, the government moved resolutely toward the gradual elimination of feudal restrictions and Confucian ranks (*samurai*, peasant, artisan, and merchant). However, the undercurrent of feudalism remained an undeniable aspect of the period, particularly in law. For instance, different types of punishment were applied to the same crime, depending on whether the guilty party was *kazoku, shizoku, heimin,* or a government official. This kind of discriminatory practice was sanctioned by the 1870 Essence of the New Criminal Code and Amended Criminal Code and Statutes of 1873, both of which showed the influence of the ancient Chinese legal system. Status distinctions in criminal law were not eliminated until the promulgation of the Penal Code in 1882.

Likewise, government economic reforms did not completely extirpate feudal influences. Although the land system was reformed with the revision of the tax law, the practice of landowners' extracting an exorbitantly high fraction of their tenants' production as rent in kind continued unabated. Furthermore, although tax payments were now made to the government in cash, there was little change from the high *nengu* tax rates of the feudal era and little reduction in the percentage of government revenues derived from agricultural production. Modern industry, mostly manufacturing, was run largely by the government itself. In short, the early

Meiji years were characterized by a centralized and authoritarian *ritsuryō* regime of the Chinese style, superimposed on a feudal base. The conscript army was thought of as the emperor's army, and government officials as the emperor's officials. This was the government that committed Japan to building a "wealthy country and strong military" (*fukoku kyōhei*) and to modernizing its society.

9. Foreign Policies of the Meiji Government

The early Meiji government attempted to restore the traditional diplomacy of parity with Korea but received a rebuff which led to Saigo's 1873 plan for a punitive expedition. In 1875, a Japanese warship was bombarded off Kanghwa Island in Korea, and the Japanese government took that opportunity to conclude a treaty of amity with Korea in the following year.

In the Edo era, there had been active trade relations between the merchants of China and Japan but no diplomatic relations between the two countries. The Meiji government, therefore, signed a Japan-China Amity Treaty on equal terms in 1871.

Japan's territorial claims were among the most important diplomatic issues of the early Meiji period. Both Japan and Russia claimed Sakhalin Island (Karafuto), but, as a result of negotiations between the two countries in 1875, Japan gave up its claim in exchange for sovereignty over the Kurile Islands (Chishima). Both China and Japan claimed the Ryūkyū (Loochoo) Islands, whose ruler, during the Edo era, had acknowledged the sovereignty of both powers. The Meiji government insisted that the archipelago was Japanese territory, and in 1879, Ryūkyū *han* was abolished and Okinawa Prefecture (*ken*) established in its place. The Bonin (Ogasawara) Islands had long been recognized as Japanese territory by the United States. The British felt otherwise, but in 1876 Japan declared them as its own.

B. Constitutional Monarchy
Middle Phase, Meiji Constitution, 1882–1931

1. The Making of the Constitution and the Beginning of Parliamentary Government

In 1881, an imperial edict stated that a parliament would be opened in 1890. Itō Hirobumi was sent to Europe in 1882 to study the constitutions of other countries. In 1881, Iwakura Tomomi, the *udaijin*, had drawn up a set of general principles and a commentary supporting a monarchical constitution like that of Prussia. His recommendations were almost all adopted in the Meiji Constitution. Itō, according to Iwakura's recommendation, studied with R. von Gneist and A. Mosse of Germany, and with L. von. Stein of Austria. When he returned to Japan in 1883, Ōkuma had resigned and Iwakura had died, leaving Itō the sole major figure on the political scene. In 1884 he established the Seido Torishirabe Kyoku (Institutions Research Bureau), and became its director. With the assistance of Inoue Kowashi, Itō Miyoji, and Kaneko Kentarō, he made preparations in secret for drawing up the constitution and supplementary laws. In the same year, in anticipation of the opening of an upper house, the *Kazoku Rei* (Law of Nobility) was promulgated, establishing the five aristocratic titles of prince, marquis, count, viscount, and baron. In 1885, the *dajōkan* was abolished and its authority transferred to a cabinet (*naikaku*) on the European model. Under the *dajōkan* system, the *dajōdaijin*, together with the *sadaijin* and *udaijin*, were seen as assisting the emperor in the conduct of state affairs, and the various ministry heads as mere bureaucratic subordinates. The new cabinet was a collegial decision-making body made up of a prime minister and ministers of foreign affairs, home affairs, finance, army, navy, justice, education, agriculture and commerce, and communications. In the cabinet, all these ministers took part in making national policies, and outside it, each discharged the duties of his specific branch. The new system also institutionalized a clear distinction between the government and the imperial court itself. An additional ministry, of the imperial household (*kunai*), was established outside the cabinet, and Sanjō Sanetomi, who had been *dajōdaijin*, was named minister (*naidaijin*). Sanjō was thus in charge of liaison between the court and the government. A large amount of state property was also transferred to the imperial household at about the same time. The office of prime minister was assumed by Itō Hirobumi. The elevation of Itō, a man of lower-rank *samurai* origins, to this post amazed the people of the time.

As the government carried out these preparations for the promulgation of the constitution, corresponding political movements were in progress among the people. The Liberal Party (Jiyūtō) was founded in 1881 and the Constitutional Imperial Rule Party (Rikken Teiseitō) in 1882. These parties, however, were dissolved in 1883 and 1884, respectively, as several conditions made it difficult for parties to survive. The government repressed political movements, both directly and indirectly, using both pressure and persuasion. The parties themselves engaged in internecine power struggles. Most important, Liberal Party headquarters was unable to restrain its local members from participating in riots by poor farmers, which broke out in several areas due to the unfavorable economic conditions created by the government's deflationary policies. Even though the parties could not continue, however, riots by local liberals went on. In 1887, great numbers of people memorialized the government on such topics as treaty revision, freedom of speech and assembly, and reduction of taxes. Gotō Shōjirō and others revived the party movement by organizing the opposition into a "Great Coalition" (Daidō Danketsu). Disorder in the capital followed, and in the same year, the Peace Preservation Law (Hoan Jōrei) was promulgated, enabling the government to expel people's rights advocates from Tokyo, requiring them to remain at a distance of more than three ri (about 12 kilometers) from the capital.

In 1888, the Privy Council (Sūmitsuin) was established. Itō Hirobumi was appointed its president and started examining the draft constitution that had been in preparation since the end of 1885. In anticipation of the promulgation of the Constitution, local autonomy was established through a system of shi (cities) and chō-son (towns and villages), enacted in 1888 and one of fu-ken (prefectures) and gun (counties), enacted in 1890. On February 11, 1889, the Constitution was promulgated. It was, as we have seen, a monarchic constitution, based on Iwakura's principles and opinions. The drafting was mainly the work of Inoue Kowashi and K. F. H. Roesler, a German.

The Constitution went into effect on November 29, 1890, the day the First Imperial Diet was convened. It comprised 76 articles in seven chapters. It was a monarchic constitution in the Prussian style, but it was simply worded and was characterized by elasticity. It stated that the Japanese empire was to be ruled by the emperor (of lineage unbroken through the ages) according to the articles of the Constitution. All three branches of the government —executive, legislative, and judicial—were to be presided over by the emperor. A great many things were included in the imperial prerogative and therefore did not require the consent of the Diet. An especially severe restriction on the Diet's fiscal authority was imposed by the rule stipulating that the previous year's budget went into effect automatically if the Diet failed to approve a new one. Laws could not be passed without Diet approval, but constitutional amendments could be proposed by the emperor alone. The ruler was also given broad powers to issue special emergency ordinances (*kinkyū meirei*), independent supplementary ordinances (*dokuritsu meirei*) and ordinances delegating his authority to subordinates (*inin meirei*). The constitution also laid down rules concerning the rights and duties of the people, but these dealt only with the relation of the people to the nation, and ideas of fundamental human rights were not strongly articulated. Instead, the freedoms granted were nearly all made subject to whatever limitations the law might determine. The Imperial Diet was bicameral, consisting of the House of Representatives, elected by the nation at large, and the House of Peers, made up of *kazoku* (nobility), who were the bulwarks of the Imperial House, and officially nominated members. Except for the priority recognized for the House of Representatives in the debates on the budget, the two houses had equal rights. The judicial power was independent, but the right to appoint or dismiss judges was held by the Minister of Justice. Supreme command of the army and the navy rested with the emperor and, in accordance with earlier tradition, was placed outside the scope of the ministers' power to advise the ruler; this practice was ultimately to lead to military dictatorship.

Since this Meiji Constitution was characterized by elasticity, it admitted of different interpretations, and many changes should be noted in the history of its operation. For instance, in the minds of the original makers of the Constitution the formation and continuation of the Cabinet depended on the emperor's confidence and were to have nothing to do with the Diet. Later, however, it became customary for the Cabinet to be formed by political parties. Also, the draftsmen had intended that there should be property restrictions on voting, but the Constitution relegated the matter to law and contained no clear article on it, thus enabling the nation to win universal male suffrage in 1925.

Together with the Constitution, the Imperial House Law (*Kō-shitsu Tenpan*) and such supplementary laws as the Diet Law, the House of Representatives Election Law, and the Imperial Ordinance on the House of Peers were issued.

In 1890, the members of the nobility elected their representatives to the House of Peers, and additional representatives were nominated by the emperor. A general election for the House of Representatives was held,* and in November of that year the First Imperial Diet was opened. A majority of the elected members of the House of Representatives were from either the Liberal Party (Jiyūtō) or the Constitutional Reform Party (Rikken Kaishintō), and thus stood to some degree in opposition to the government. The government was represented by the Cabinet under Yamagata Aritomo. The first Diet session ended in comparative peace.

The Matsukata (Masayoshi) Cabinet that followed Yamagata's engaged in wide-scale bribery and intimidation before the general election of 1892. This became the pattern for the Satsuma-Chōshū clique cabinets in dealing with the political party opposition: combining repression and harassment with conciliation. For their part, the parties attacked the government in the only way open to them: by drastically cutting government budgets in the House of Representatives.

2. Treaty Revision

"Enriching the country and strengthening the army" (*fukoku kyōhei*) and "increasing production and encouraging industry" (*shokusan kōgyō*), the mottos of the government since the early

---

* This was called a general election, but in fact only those who paid a national tax of 15 yen or more were able to vote. Such taxpayers were only 1.1 percent of the nation's total population—about 450,000 persons.

The House of Representatives Election Law, officially announced on the same day as the Constitution, laid down the following voting qualifications for Japanese subjects:

(1) To be at least twenty-five years of age,

(2) To have resided in the prefecture of his domicile for one year previous to the registration of voters, and

(3) To have been paying, in his domiciliary prefecture, a direct national tax of 15 yen or more. As the Meiji Consitution left the matter of voter qualification to the election laws, they could be changed without constitutional amendment.

years of Meiji, represented its efforts to raise the status of Japan to the level of the advanced countries of Europe and North America. One of the principal objectives was the revision of the unequal treaties with the European Powers.

Terajima Munenori, minister of foreign affairs, negotiated in 1876 to recover tariff rights* but did not succeed. Inoue Kaoru, who followed him as foreign minister, endeavored to put domestic law in good order as the first step, and encouraged the trend toward Europeanization often referred to as the "Rokumeikan Age," but his excessive emphasis on Europeanization and his agreement to appoint foreigners as judges aroused popular criticism. In 1888, Ōkuma Shigenobu, then foreign minister, took responsibility for negotiating treaty revision. He agreed to the appointment of foreigners to the Supreme Court (*daishin'in*), and this, too, met such violent opposition that he had to resign. In the meantime, however, the nation's laws were being put in better form. Helped by these developments, Mutsu Munemitsu, who became foreign minister in 1892, talked with foreign governments about equal treaties. First he won the consent of England, with whom he concluded a revised treaty in 1894, and followed this success with similar treaties with other countries. All of the new treaties took effect in 1899. However, Japan had to wait until 1911 for the complete recovery of tariff autonomy.

3. The Compilation of Codes

The first codes compiled by the Meiji government were the Essence of the New Criminal Code (*Shinritsu Kōryō*), promulgated in 1870 and based on Chinese legal principles, and the Amended Criminal Code and Statutes (*Kaitei Ritsurei*) of 1873, in the same legal tradition. At the same time, however, the government was working toward a uniform civil code for the entire country. Later, the compilation of civil and other legal codes was speeded up in order to facilitate treaty revision. The first such codes to be drafted were based on French jurisprudence, but after the promulgation of the Constitution the German influence became increasingly dominant. The Criminal Code of 1880 (usually referred to as the Old Criminal

*The treaties concluded between the *bakufu* and the Five Powers in 1858 imposed an "agreed custom rate" which no one power could alter without the consent of the others, and this disadvantageous condition was again imposed on Japan by the tariff revision agreement of 1866.

Code) (*Kyū-kei Hō*) and the Code of Criminal Procedure (*Chizai Hō*) enacted in the same year were both in the French tradition, and were put into force in 1882. These were Japan's first modern legal codes and are especially noteworthy in that they abolished all differences in treatment based on social status and also established the modern principle of determination of criminal sanction by legal rule. This legislation, then, marked an important step in the modernization of Japan and constitutes one reason why the year 1882 is taken here as the dividing line between the early and middle stages of the modern period.

The most notable accomplishment in this field, however, was the compilation of a civil code. The civil code compiled by the French legal advisor G. E. Boissonade (the Old Civil Code, *Kyū-minpō*), promulgated in 1890, was to take effect in 1893. It was attacked by conservatives, however, on the grounds that it ignored established Japanese custom and that it was poorly drafted. Enforcement was therefore postponed, and the code was revised on the model of German civil law by the legal scholars Ume Kenjirō, Hozumi Nobushige, and Tomii Masaaki, resulting in the New Civil Code, which went into effect in 1898.

The Commercial Code was compiled by K.F.H. Roesler, a German, but its enforcement too (except for one portion) was postponed until 1899. In 1890, the Code of Civil Procedure and Code of Criminal Procedure, both in the German style, were issued.

Among the more important later developments was the issuing of the New Criminal Code in 1908. This code showed strong subjectivist tendencies: judges were given wide discretion in sentencing, and suspended sentences were allowed. It remained in force until 1924, when a new Code of Criminal Procedure was put into effect. In 1929 the first five books of the Code of Civil Procedure were extensively revised, and major revisions were also made in the Commercial Code after the Meiji era.

Of all the laws of Japan, the commercial law and the code of legal procedure showed the strongest influence of foreign legal traditions. In civil law, especially the law of domestic relations and succession, the coloring of the native law of Japan was strongly evident. Like the *buke* law of the Edo era, Meiji civil law recognized strong rights for the head of the household and authorized the system of male primogeniture. In marriage, the principle of supremacy of the husband was confirmed. All these persistent features from the pre-modern age made possible the survival of various feudal customs, and constituted a major characteristic of Japan's modern society.

4. Changes in Party Government

Itō Hirobumi, the "author" of the Constitution, did not approve of party government, in which the leader of the majority party becomes the prime minister. But the actual progress of parliamentary government made it impossible to disregard the power of political parties. As a result of Japan's victory in the war with China in 1894–95, Japan's international status was raised. Internally, in 1897, the gold standard was established; industrial capitalism was developing, and with it the power of political parties increased. In 1898 the first political party cabinet in Japan was born, although it lasted for only four months. Itō, realizing the growing importance of political parties, organized, in 1900, the Rikken Seiyūkai (Friends of Constitutional Government) out of the Constitutional Government Party (Kenseitō), which had developed from the old Liberal Party (Jiyūtō), becoming its president ten years after the convocation of the first Diet. The fourth Itō Cabinet, organized in the same year, was therefore a Seiyūkai cabinet. This cabinet, however, was soon brought down by opposition from the House of Peers, the citadel of the bureaucracy, and it was followed by cabinets that were not supported by political parties.

Then, from about the time when the First World War entered its latter phase, the tide of democracy which was spreading throughout the world had its day also in Japan. In 1918, when the Terauchi Cabinet was overthrown by the *kome-sōdō* ("rice riot" protesting sharply rising commodity prices), Hara Satoshi (Kei), president of the Seiyūkai, seized his chance and formed a government with a pure party cabinet. Hara was the first *heimin* (commoner) and member of the House of Representatives to head a cabinet. Though he had been a member of the old Jiyūtō, he had become quite conservative; the Kenseikai (Constitutional Government Association), which had developed from the old Progressive Party (Kaishintō), was more progressive. The Kenseikai demanded universal suffrage, but the Hara Cabinet insisted that the time for this had not yet come. In 1924, a new cabinet was organized by members of the House of Peers with Kiyoura Keigo as prime minister, and three lower house groups formed a "Coalition of Three in Defense of the Constitution" (*Goken Sampa*). This coalition, composed of the Seiyūkai, the Kenseikai, and the Reform Club (Kakushin Kurabu) of Inukai Tsuyoshi and others, won the support of public opinion and forced the Kiyoura Cabinet to resign. The new prime minister was Katō Takaaki, president of the Kenseikai, and other cabinet members were drawn from the three groups in the coalition. Under this cabinet, in 1925, a universal male suffrage law was passed in the Diet. This government also acted decisively in the areas of administrative and financial retrenchment, particularly in the reduction of armaments. In the eight years that passed between this time and the fall of the Seiyūkai Cabinet of Inukai Tsuyoshi in 1932, cabinets were formed in turn by the activist Seiyūkai and the more passive Kenseikai (or—as it was called after incorporating the Seiyū Hontō, a Seiyūkai splinter group—the Minseitō or People's Government Party), depending on which could get majority support in the Diet. There was thus a sequence of five cabinets selected in accordance with what was considered to be orthodox constitutional procedure.

The universal suffrage law gave the right to vote to all men in their 25th year or older, and all men in their 30th year or older could be candidates for election. This quadrupled the preexisting electorate, and in 1928 the first general election according to the universal suffrage law was held. The majority of the seats were occupied by the members of Seiyūkai and Kenseikai, but the proletarian parties also obtained some seats.

In this way, under the party cabinets, curbs were gradually being put on the power of the military cliques and the bureaucracy that had supplanted the old *han* cliques. Reduction of armaments was carried out, and conciliatory policies were taken in international relations. The armament reduction—above all the London Treaty of Naval Disarmament of 1930—was received with great dissatisfaction by the navy and intensified the militarists' distrust of party government. Premier Hamaguchi, responsible for these developments, was shot by a rightist group in 1930. The army, under Premier Tanaka's Seiyūkai Cabinet, in 1927, sent expeditionary forces to Shantung Province, China, to thwart the Chinese

revolutionary forces' march northward, alleging the need to protect resident Japanese. The following year Chang Tso-lin, warlord
of Manchuria, was bombed to death by the Japanese Kwantung
Army. These events marked the beginning of the dictatorship
of the militarists.

The economy remained in a state of chronic depression after the
panic following World War I. Recovery was made even more difficult by the Great Kantō Earthquake of 1923 and a bank panic in
1927. The political parties, in the meantime, became unscrupulous
in their quest for power and allied themselves with the *zaibatsu*
(the Seiyūkai with Mitsui, the Kenseikai with Mitsubishi). Party
government as a result gradually became corrupted.

Regarding the appointment of the prime minister, it was the
custom in early years for the leader of the outgoing cabinet to
recommend to the emperor the man to be his successor, but by
about 1900 it became the rule for the *genrō* (elder statesmen) to
recommend the prospective premier. Party government, in fact,
meant the nomination by a *genrō* to the emperor of the leader of the
majority party as the next premier.

Japan's physical territory was expanding steadily during this
period. As a result of the Sino-Japanese War of 1894–95, Taiwan
(Formosa) and the Penghus (the Pescadores) were given by China
to Japan; the Russo-Japanese War of 1904–5 resulted in half of
Sakhalin Island (from the 50° latitude southward) being ceded to
Japan by Russia. In 1910 Korea was annexed. After World War
I, the South Sea Islands north of the equator that had been
German territory were placed under the mandate of Japan.

C. The Decay of Constitutional Monarchy
Final Phase, 1931–1945

1. From the Manchurian Incident to the China Incident

Prime Minister Hamaguchi was shot in 1930 and died the next
year. Ignoring the government's policy of non-proliferation of
warfare, the military forces in 1931 took over the whole of Manchuria and established the entity called Manchukuo in March
of 1932. In May of the same year, a group of naval officers and
noncommissioned officers, with the aim of establishing a military

government, assaulted the official residence of the prime minister and killed Inukai Tsuyoshi, premier and president of the Seiyūkai, in what is known as the May 15 Incident. The incident brought an end to party government, and Admiral Saitō Makoto became prime minister in the first of a series of so-called "National Unity" cabinets not based on political parties.

The League of Nations, in answer to an appeal from the Chinese government, sent a survey team to Manchuria. The team declared the actions of Japan in Manchuria to be aggressive, and stated that the foundation of Manchukuo was not (as Japan claimed) a voluntary movement for independence. It concluded that, although Japan's special interests in Manchuria should be recognized, all its armed forces should be withdrawn. This report was supported by the League's general session of 1933, and so Japan decided to withdraw from the League, of which it had been a member since its establishment.

Japan pursued an independent course in foreign policy and became more and more isolated internationally. In 1934 the effective period of the Washington Naval Treaty expired, and Japan announced its abrogation. At the naval disarmament conference held in London at the end of 1935, Japan insisted on possessing a navy equal in size to those of Britain and the U.S.; when its demands were not met, Japan withdrew from the conference.

Saitō Makoto was followed as prime minister by Admiral Okada Keisuke. These men and their cabinets were fairly liberal in policy; some military officers, dissatisfied with them, resorted to violence to sweep away the liberalistic tendency in politics. About a dozen officers of the army's First Division, leading more than a thousand soldiers, rose in rebellion in 1936, attacked the prime minister's official residence and other places, and occupied the central area of Tokyo. Premier Okada narrowly escaped death, but several other high officials, including Saitō Makoto, then *naidaijin*, were assassinated. The attack is known as the February 26 Incident.

This uprising was soon put down, but the militarists took advantage of it to expand their influence and role in the government. At the end of the year, in response to pressure from the army, an anti-Comintern pact was concluded with Germany; it professed a joint defense against communism, in order to resist the threat of the Soviet Union. In 1937, this pact was expanded to include Italy.

The Kwantung army, encouraged by its success in Manchuria, extended its war front from North China to Central China and then to South China, despite the government's localization policy. This undeclared war is known as *Nisshi jihen*, or the China Incident.

2. The National General Mobilization Act and the Imperial Rule Assistance Association

With this expansion of the battle front, the munitions industry became increasingly active. The embargo on the export of gold, lifted by the Hamaguchi Cabinet in 1930, was revived in 1931. Japan's exports increased, and the economy thrived at first, but the prolonged warfare began to take its toll financially and brought about a shortage of goods. Wartime control more and more affected the life of the nation.

The government, in an effort to accomplish its war objectives at whatever cost, issued a declaration of a New Order in East Asia in 1938, and demanded the "total mobilization of the national spirit" by issuing the National General Mobilization Act, which in effect deprived the nation of the freedom of speech. This law endowed the government with the power to mobilize the total power of the nation, in wartime and in times of emergency equivalent to war, without having to obtain the approval of the Imperial Diet. It was a law practically nullifying the function of the Diet. There were protests against this virtual nullification of the function of the Diet from both the Seiyūkai and the Minseitō, but the demurring voices were suppressed by the high-handedness of the militarists, and the Diet passed the measure without amendment. In 1939, the Personal Service Drafting Law (*Chōyō Rei*) was issued.

With the outbreak of World War II in 1939, the Abe (Nobuyuki) Cabinet declared that Japan would not interfere with the war in Europe. Under the next cabinet, however—that of Admiral Yonai Mitsumasa—the army insisted on concluding a strong military alliance with Germany. The prime minister and the navy objected to it, but a military alliance with Germany and Italy was formally concluded by the second Konoe (Fumimaro) Cabinet in 1940. In the same year, Foreign Minister Matsuoka Yōsuke declared the establishment of the Greater East Asia Co-Prosperity Sphere (*Daitōa Kyōeiken*).

Konoe in October 1940 established the *Taisei Yokusan Kai* (Imperial Rule Assistance Association) and became its president. This was the outcome of the movement for a new order which had been evolving around Konoe since June of that year. All the political parties—Seiyūkai, Minseitō, Kokumin Dōmei, Shakai Taishūtō—were now dissolved. With the formation of the *Taisei Yokusan Kai*, the ultra-partisan national movement desired by the militarists had materialized, and the political parties, which had relinquished their right to deliberate on state affairs in the Diet by their passage of the National General Mobilization Act, had lost their own *raison d'être*. Constitutional government—that is, governments formed by the parties—had disappeared, and the Meiji Constitution had lost its function as fundamental law. All labor unions were dissolved, and the *Dai Nihon Sangyō Hōkoku Kai* (Japanese Association of Industrialists' Service to the State) was formed to take their place.

Finally, in December 1941, with the attack of the Japanese navy on Pearl Harbor, Hawaii, the Pacific War began. The Japanese armed forces fared well in the beginning, but suffered a serious setback in the sea battle off Midway in June 1942. In May 1945, Germany, Japan's ally in Europe, surrendered unconditionally to the Allied Powers. In June, all the land forces in Okinawa were destroyed. While the militarists were announcing the imminence of the decisive battle on the mainland of Japan, the Potsdam Declaration was published on July 26, 1945, by the United States, Britain, and France (later joined by the Soviet Union); the Declaration prescribed the final conditions for Japan's surrender. The Japanese government at first ignored it, but after the aerial attacks on Hiroshima (August 6) and on Nagasaki (August 9), in which atomic bombs were used, and the sudden declaration of war on Japan by the Soviet Union followed by the Soviet invasion of North Manchuria and northern Korea, the Suzuki (Kantaro) Cabinet notified the Allied forces on August 14 of Japan's decision to accept the Declaration. On August 15, 1945, the emperor's recorded message on the termination of the war was broadcast to the nation. On August 30, General Douglas MacArthur of the U.S. arrived at Atsugi Airport, and the occupation of Japan by the Allied Powers began.

3. Economic Control

When the China Incident occurred in 1937, the government saw the urgent need to increase munitions production and made all resources, funds, and imports subservient to the arms industry. The sudden growth of the munitions industry caused inflation, and prices began to rise. With the outbreak of World War II in September 1939, the government, using the powers given it by the National General Mobilization Act, enforced price-control regulations in an attempt to check the rise of prices. Commercial and industrial syndicates were formed all over the nation, and all enterprises were placed under government control.

The Pacific War began under these circumstances. After the United States became Japan's main enemy, all materials, funds, and labor were made to serve the fighting power of Japan. Private enterprises were suppressed, and a number of semi-governmental, semi-private companies were created. Since Japan had limited resources for a war of this scale, ordinary consumption was greatly restricted, and strong controls were applied, even to food and clothing.

4. Decay of Constitutional Monarchy

In terms of political institutions, the fourteen years from the Manchurian Incident (1931) to the end of the Pacific War (1945) was a period marked by the decay of constitutional monarchy.

The emperor was held in awe as a divinity incarnate (*arahito-gami*), and was used by the militarists as a shield against criticism of their wrongful and illegal acts. But since the Meiji Constitution was still in effect, the emperor was in fact the ruler of the nation, and his termination of the Pacific War in 1945 by his own decision was the last and greatest glory achieved by the emperor system under the Meiji Constitution.

The Meiji Constitution, although it did not anticipate the growth of party cabinets, expected the Diet to function properly as a legislative organ. From the middle of the Taishō era to the early Shōwa years, party cabinets were formed one after another, but after 1932 the party system ceased to function, and the National General Mobilization Act deprived the Diet of much of its right to deliberate on state affairs. After 1942, when the *Yokusan Seiji Kai* (Political Assistance Association) was formed, and *yokusan giin* (cooperative Diet members) were elected, the Diet became a puppet legislature which applauded every move of the government. Freedoms of speech, assembly, and publication guaranteed by the Meiji Constitution were taken away; security of ownership was disregarded; and under the controlled economy, freedom to enter into contracts was severely restricted.

Thus, the Meiji Constitution still existed, in name only, during the war years. However, even the militarists did not try to abolish the Constitution. They had no need to do so, for anything could be accomplished by invoking the emperor's authority. By making full use of the prerogative of supreme command acknowledged by the Constitution, the militarists could have their own way.

CHAPTER 6

CONSTITUTIONAL DEMOCRACY

Gendai, or Contemporary Period, 1945–present

1. The Allied Occupation and Control of Japan

Within two weeks of Japan's surrender, Allied forces began landing in Japan to occupy the country. On October 2, 1945, General Headquarters (GHQ) of the Allied Powers was formally established in Tokyo under the direction of Supreme Commander for the Allied Powers (SCAP) General Douglas MacArthur. MacArthur retained this post until 1951, when he was replaced by another American, General Matthew Ridgeway. Two multinational bodies were established to provide MacArthur with guidelines for the occupation: the Far Eastern Commission (FEC) in Washington, D.C., and the Allied Council for Japan in Tokyo. The FEC comprised representatives from eleven of the Allied Powers, including the United States, Great Britain, France, and the Soviet Union. It was responsible for determining the powers' policies, and the supreme commander was charged with implementing its decisions. The Allied Council for Japan was a smaller body, consisting of representatives from the United States, Great Britain, the Soviet Union, and China, and was an advisory organ for the supreme commander. The overall administration was conducted through the government of Japan, which continued to function during the Allied occupation. They were made subordinate to the supreme commander, and they were responsible for carrying out the directives and recommendations transmitted to them from his office.

2. Policies of the Allied Occupation

The occupation policies of the Allied Powers in Japan were directed toward the elimination of "feudal and militaristic" elements from Japanese society, and the promotion of modern freedom and peace.

a) Political Reforms. Japan's armed forces were disarmed and then disbanded. War criminals were arrested, tried, and punished by Allied military tribunals in the name of civilization. Militarists, ultranationalists, and war leaders were purged for a time from public office and educational positions. Those imprisoned for political crimes during the war were released, and all laws curbing freedom of speech, assembly, and association—in particular, the Peace Preservation Law—were repealed. The right of women to vote and hold public office was recognized, even before constitutional reform, and in the 1946 general election thirty-nine women were elected to serve in the Lower House of the Diet.

The police system was reformed: police were confined to strictly defined duties and prevented from engaging in many of the wide-ranging surveillance and political activities which had so intimidated the citizenry before the surrender. Further measures were taken to promote the decentralization and democratization of the police system. The older centralized system was abolished, and all cities, towns, and villages with populations of five thousand or more were directed to establish their own police forces. The new system, however, had a dual structure: all areas not under the jurisdiction of municipal government police were placed under a network of national regional police, supported by the national budget. Each unit (city, town, or village, or, in the case of the national regional police, the prefecture) was placed under a Public Safety Commission (*Kōan Iinkai*), none of whose commissioners could be civil servants. Most of the Allied forces stationed in Japan were sent to Korea in 1950, when war began in that country. To fill the vacuum created by their departure, the Occupation authorities approved the creation of a Police Reserve Corps (*Keisatsu Yobitai*).

The most important political reform, of course, was the promulgation of the new constitution, which is discussed in the following section.

b) Social and Economic Reforms. The supreme commander issued a number of directives to the Japanese government aimed at eliminating "feudal elements" from Japan's society and economy. The directives were also intended to modernize and democratize Japanese society, and in fact their implementation effected a radical transformation of Japan's social structure.

Two directives resulted in the drafting of a Labor Union Law (*Rōdō Kumiai Hō*) and a Labor Standards Law (*Rōdō Kijun Hō*), which established the legal right of workers to organize and defined minimum legal conditions of employment. In essence, these laws transformed Japan's laborers into modern wage-earners.

Another important directive was issued for the purpose of breaking up the *zaibatsu*. These combines, which included Mitsui, Mitsubishi, Sumitomo, and Yasuda, played a monopolistic role in various Japanese industries, especially the armaments industry; they had promoted and financed the war and endangered the livelihood of the people. The Antimonopoly Law (*Dokusen Kinshi Hō*) and the Deconcentration Law (*Shūchū Haijo Hō*) were also intended to break up these huge economic combines.

The final area of significant economic change was of course the land reform. Land reform was in fact carried out in two stages, in 1945 and 1946. The government first bought up arable land which was not being cultivated by its owners and sold it back cheaply to the tenants who had been working it. Where tenancy survived this program, the government ordered all rents to be paid in cash. In the second phase of the reform, landowners who lived in the villages but did not cultivate their own lands were forbidden to personally own more than one *chō* (two and one-half acres) of land. This measure liberated 2 million of the 2.6 million hectares of cultivated land in the country from landlord control. The feudal relationship between landlord and tenant was thus dissolved everywhere, and a major step forward was taken toward democratizing the agrarian village. This land reform was unique in Japanese history, for it originated in the recommendations of a foreign source, but it nonetheless stands along with the Taika Reform and the *taikō kenchi* as one of Japan's three great agrarian reforms.

3. Establishment of a New Japanese Constitution

The various reforms discussed above were based on Article X of the Potsdam Declaration, which read:

The Japanese Government shall remove all obstacles to the revival and strengthening of democratic tendencies among the Japanese people. Freedom of speech, of religion and of thought, as well as respect for the fundamental human rights shall be established.

These principles, combined with a new definition of the emperor as a non-divine symbol of the Japanese nation (as he was declared to be in an imperial rescript on January 1, 1946), became the basic outline of a new democratic Japanese constitution. The draft of the constitution originated in the General Headquarters of the occupation authority, and it underwent minor revisions at the hands of the Japanese government. In order to issue it, however, SCAP decided to treat the new charter as a formal revision of the Meiji Constitution, and consequently, the amendment procedures of the old constitution were followed meticulously. After the emperor's approval had been formally obtained, the new constitution was submitted to the Privy Council for examination. It was then referred to both houses of the Diet, where it was approved with minor revisions. Subsequently it was sent back to the Privy Council for approval, and to the emperor for imperial sanction. The constitution was finally adopted on November 3, 1946, and came into effect exactly six months later.

The new Constitution of Japan contains 11 chapters and 103 articles. Sovereignty is vested in the people while the emperor is regarded simply as the symbol of state and of the unity of the people. The Constitution establishes basic human rights in a Bill of Rights and explicitly renounces the sovereign right of the nation to wage war. It establishes a bicameral Diet as the highest organ of national authority, with a lower house, called the House of Representatives, and a House of Councilors (both popularly elected). Executive power is vested in the cabinet, which is responsible to the Diet. The judicial branch of government is separated from the other two branches in an independent court system. The 1947 constitution gives clear encouragement to local self-government in provisions directed toward political and administrative decentralization.

Of all these provisions, those related to the guarantee of fundamental human rights are particularly notable. The rights of the individual and the equality of the sexes in family life are given legal recognition. Hence, the old primogenitural family system and the privileged position of the household head have been rejected legally, while the principles of freedom to marry, equal status between sexes, and divisible inheritance have been given a legal foundation. The Constitution gives detailed guarantees of personal freedom, including the right to live, to receive education, to work, and to organize. The reforms contained in the Constitution thus extend widely into the public and personal lives of Japanese citizens.

4. Restoration of National Independence

Japan finally signed a peace treaty ending World War II at the San Francisco Peace Conference in September 1951. Forty-nine countries were represented at the conference, and Prime Minister Yoshida Shigeru served as Japan's plenipotentiary delegate. Serious controversy over whether it was appropriate to conclude a peace treaty which did not receive the approval of all belligerents, or whether a peace treaty signed by all parties (including the Soviet Union) was necessary, was resolved in favor of the former course. The treaty restored Japan's sovereignty to the Japanese people and recognized Japan as a member of the community of nations. A United States–Japan security agreement was concluded simultaneously with the signing of the peace treaty, authorizing the continued presence of American forces on Japanese soil. This agreement and the peace treaty went into effect in April 1952, and ever since that time, the American bases in Japan have been a constant source of domestic controversy.

By virtue of the San Francisco Peace Treaty, Japan relinquished its rights in Taiwan, the Pescadores, the Northern Kuriles, Sakhalin, and the islands of the South Pacific, and recognized the independence of Korea. Controversy still exists over whether Japanese sovereignty extends to certain of the southernmost islands in the Kurile chain; this issue, left unclear in the San Francisco Treaty, developed into a protracted territorial dispute obstructing the conclusion of a peace treaty formally ending the war with the USSR.

CHRONOLOGICAL TABLE

Western Calendar Year	Japanese Calendar Year	Emperor	Regent, Shōgun, etc.	Events
		ARCHAIC	PERIOD	(JŌDAI)
108 B.C.				Emperor Wu Ti, of the Former Han dynasty, establishes in Korea the four commanderies of Lo-Lang, Chen-Fan, Lin-T'un, and Hsuan-T'u. Beyond these, in Japan, according to the *Han History,* lie "over one hundred" separate countries.
A.D. 25				Later Han dynasty established in China.
57				The Na country of Wa sends an embassy to Emperor Kuang-Wu of the Later Han, and is granted a seal.
				Two cultural spheres coexist in Japan, one characterized by bronze bells and the other by bronze swords and spears.
107				Shishō, King of Wa (or of the "country of Mendo" in Wa) and others send an embassy to the Later Han court.
				In the latter half of the second century A.D., there is "great disorder" in the country of Wa, with a number of clans warring with one another. After many years without a ruler, all agree to submit to the authority of Queen Himiko.
220				The Later Han falls, to be replaced by the three kingdoms of Wei, Wu, and Shu.
247				Himiko wars with the country of Kuna.
				Himiko dies, and a king is established whom the people will not acknowledge. Toyo, a thirteen-year-old girl of Himiko's clan, is made queen.
265				The kingdom of Wei is destroyed by the Ch'in.
266				Iyo sends an embassy to the Western Ch'in.
318				Alleged year of Emperor Sujin's death.
391				Wa armies cross the sea and defeat Paekche and Silla kingdoms (in Korea).
421				Tsan, king of Wa, sends an embassy to the Liu-Sung court in south China, becoming the first of the line of "five Wa kings" to send envoys to the south China courts.
538				Buddhism introduced to Japan.

133

Western Calendar Year	Japanese Calendar Year	Emperor	Regent, Shōgun, etc.	Events
562		Kinmei		Silla destroys the Japanese headquarters in Mimana.
572		Bidatsu	Mononobe no Moriya, Ōmuraji; Soga no Umako, Ōomi	Mononobe no Moriya appointed Ōmuraji. Soga no Umako appointed Ōomi.
587		Yōmei	Soga no Umako, Ōomi	Fall of the Mononobe uji from power.
592		Sushun	Soga no Umako, Ōomi	Enthronement of Empress Suiko.
593		Empress Suiko	Soga no Umako, Ōomi	Prince Shōtoku is made crown prince and conducts the affairs of the state jointly with the Ōomi, Soga no Umako.

ANCIENT   PERIOD   (JŌSEI)

603		Empress Suiko	Prince Shōtoku; Soga no Umako, Ōomi	Twelve-tier system of court ranks established.
604		Empress Suiko	Prince Shōtoku; Soga no Umako, Ōomi	Seventeen-article constitution announced.
608		Empress Suiko	Prince Shōtoku; Soga no Umako, Ōomi	Ono no Imoko sent as ambassador to Sui court, representing the "Emperor of the East," according to Japanese accounts.
623		Empress Suiko		Kusushi no Enichi and other students return from T'ang China and praise the excellence of Chinese administration and law.
643		Empress Kōgyoku	Soga no Emishi	On his own authority, Soga no Emishi grants a purple cap to his son Iruka and appoints him Ōomi.
645	Taika 1	Kōtoku	Abe no Uchimaro, Sadaijin	The Soga uji destroyed; emperor Kōtoku enthroned; sadaijin (minister of the left), udaijin (minister of the right) and naidaijin (inner minister) appointed; oath of loyalty sworn under the great tsuki (pandanus) tree, Taika era proclaimed; governors dispatched to eastern provinces.
646	Taika 2	Kōtoku	Abe no Uchimaro, Sadaijin	Taika reform edict.
649	Taika 5	Kōtoku	Kose no Tokudako, Sadaijin	The "eight ministries and one hundred official posts" of government established.
663	Tenchi "provisional" 3rd year	Tenchi		Japanese naval force defeated by the T'ang at the Kum River Estuary (Hakuson kō) in Korea.
668		Tenchi	Prince Ōama, Kōtaitei	Emperor Tenchi formally enthroned; Prince Ōama made "brother imperial" (i.e., presumative successor); Ōmi ryō enacted during this year.

Western Calendar Year	Japanese Calendar Year	Emperor	Regent, Shōgun, etc.	Events
670		Tenchi	Prince Ōama, Kōtaitei	First nationwide census (kōgo no nenjaku).
671		Tenchi	Prince Ōama, Kataitei; Prince Ōtomo, Daijō-daijin	Prince Ōtomo made minister of state (daijō-daijin); Emperor Tenchi offers succession to Prince Ōama, but Ōama retires to Yoshino.
672		Kōbun		The "Jinshin uprising" (of Prince Ōama, the future Emperor Tenmu).
673		Tenmu		Edict issued proclaiming ability as basis for choice of officials.
681		Tenmu		Edict announcing the compilation of ritsuryō and other laws; Prince Kusakabe named crown prince and given charge of government.
682		Tenmu	Prince Kusakabe, Sesshō	Tenmu ryō completed; persons of uncertain uji status excluded from consideration for office.
684		Tenmu		Tenmu's eight kabane proclaimed.
689		Empress Jitō		Tenmu ryō put into effect.
694		Empress Jitō		Court moves to the Fujiwara capital.
701	Taihō 1	Monmu		Taihō ritsuryō enacted.
702	Taihō 2	Monmu		Taihō ritsuryō put into effect.
710	Wadō 3	Empress Genmyō	Imperial Prince Hozumi, Governor of Daijōkan	The court moves to the Nara capital.
718	Yōrō 2	Empress Genshō	Fujiwara no Fuhito, Udaijin	Yōrō ritsuryō enacted.
722	Yōrō 6	Empress Genshō	Imperial Prince Toneri, Governor of Daijōkan	Announcement of plan to reclaim one million chō of new land for cultivation.
723	Yōrō 7	Empress Genshō	Imperial Prince Toneri, Governor of Daijōkan	Law of "three generations and a lifetime" for reclaimed fields, whereby newly opened fields (konden) were exempted from reallotment for the life of the reclaimer or, if he had provided new irrigation, three generations after his death.
745	Tenpyō 15	Shōmu	Prince Suzuka, Governor of Daijōkan	Konden eidai shizai hō, granting reclaimed lands to reclaimer in perpetuity.
757	Tenpyō Shōhō 9	Empress Kōken	Fujiwara no Toyonari, Udaijin	Yōrō ritsuryō put into effect.

Western Calendar Year	Japanese Calendar Year	Emperor	Regent, Shōgun, etc.	Events
759	Tenpyō Hōji 3	Empress Kōken	Emi no Oshi-katsu (Fujiwara no Nakamaro), Taiho (Udaijin)	Surpluses in public rice income (kugetō) permitted to be divided among provincial government officers as compensation.
765	Tempyō Jingo 1	Empress Shōtoku (same as Kōken)	Dōkyō, Daijō-daijin	Land reclamation prohibited.
772	Hōki 3	Kōnin	Ōnakatomi no Kiyomaro, Udaijin	Private land reclamation again permitted, without restriction.
784	Enryaku 3	Kanmu	Fujiwara no Korekimi, Udaijin	Construction of a new capital begins at Nagaoka.
792	Enryaku 11	Kanmu	Fujiwara no Tsugutada, Udaijin	Local militia (gundan) abolished, and provincial guards (kondei) established instead.
794	Enryaku 13	Kanmu	Fujiwara no Tsuginawa, Udaijin	Court moves into the Heian capital (modern Kyoto).
798	Enryaku 17	Kanmu	Prince Miwa, Udaijin,	Gun magistrates to be selected from those with reputations for skill and diligence (rather than simply on the basis of inheritance).
800	Enryaku 19	Kanmu	Prince Miwa, Udaijin	Land allotment made for the first time in the south Kyushu provinces of Satsuma and Ōsumi.
810	Kōnin 1	Saga	Fujiwara no Uchimaro, Udaijin	Kurōdo dokoro established and Fujiwara no Fuyutsugo made its head; Fujiwara no Kusuko's faction rebels and Fujiwara no Nakanari is executed in consequence.
811	Kōnin 2	Saga	Fujiwara no Uchimaro, Udaijin	It is ruled that when those entitled by lineage are unavailable, gun magistrates are to be selected from among the skilled and diligent.
818	Kōnin 9	Saga	Fujiwara no Sonohito, Udaijin	The death penalty is abolished, as a matter of unwritten custom, for crimes of theft.
820	Kōnin 11	Saga	Fujiwara no Fuyutsugu, Dainagon	The Kōnin kyakushiki is enacted. At about this time, the kebiishi chō is established.
824	Tenchō 1	Junna	Fujiwara no Fuyutsugu, Udaijin	The entire country now consists of sixty-six provinces and two "islands." No further administrative boundary changes were made for many centuries.
834	Jōwa 1	Ninmyō	Fujiwara no Ōtsugu, Sadaijin	Ryō no gige, a commentary by Kiyohara Natsuno, put into effect as the official interpretation of the ryō.
857	Ten'an 1	Montoku	Fujiwara no Yoshifusa, Daijōdaijin	Fujiwara no Yoshifusa made Daijōdaijin.

Western Calendar Year	Japanese Calendar Year	Emperor	Regent, Shōgun, etc.	Events
858	Ten'an 2	Seiwa	Fujiwara no Yoshifusa, *Sesshō*	Yoshifusa, the *Daijōdaijin*, becomes *sesshō* or regent (the equivalent of the later *kanpaku*).
880	Gangyō 4	Yōzei	Fujiwara no Mototsune, *Kanpaku*	*Daijōdaijin* Fujiwara no Mototsune is made regent for an emperor who has come of age.
887	Ninna 3	Uda	Fujiwara no Mototsune, *Kanpaku*	*Daijōdaijin* Mototsune acquires the title *kanpaku* (regent); this is the first time the title is used.
902	Engi 2	Daigo	Fujiwara no Tokihira, *Sadaijin*	Commendations of land to powerful families forbidden, and powerful families prohibited from occupying vacant lands; land allotment pressed forward.
927	Enchō 5	Daigo	Fujiwara no Tadahira, *Sadaijin*	*Engi shiki* (*shiki* of the Engi era) enacted.

MEDIEVAL PERIOD (CHŪSEI)

Western Calendar Year	Japanese Calendar Year	Emperor	Regent, Shōgun, etc.	Events
967	Kōhō 4	Reizei	Fujiwara no Saneyori, *Kanpaku*	*Engi shiki* put into effect. From this date onward, the *sesshō-kanpaku* regency is a permanent standing institution.
984	Eikan 2	Kazan	Fujiwara no Yoritada, *Kanpaku*	Establishment of new *shōen* forbidden.
988	Eien 2	Ichijō	Fujiwara no Kaneie, *Sesshō*	The *gun* magistrates and farmers of Owari Province accuse the provincial governor (*kokushi*), Fujiwara no Motonaga, of violating the law.
1028	Chōgen 1	Go-ichijō	Fujiwara no Yorimichi, *Kanpaku*	Rebellion of Taira no Tadatsune in Kantō area.
1040	Chōkyū 1	Go-suzaku	Fujiwara no Yorimichi, *Kanpaku*	Establishment of new *shōen* forbidden.
1068	Jiryaku 4	Go-sanjō	Fujiwara no Norimichi, *Kanpaku*	Emperor Go-sanjō enthroned.
1069	Enkyū 1	Go-sanjō	Fujiwara no Norimichi, *Kanpaku*	Establishment of new *shōen* forbidden; *shōen* certificate recording office opened.
1072	Enkyū 4	Go-sanjō	Fujiwara no Norimichi, *Kanpaku*	Emperor Go-sanjō abdicates, but carries on direct imperial rule in retirement.
1086	Ōtoku 3	Shirakawa	Fujiwara no Morozane, *Sesshō*	Emperor Shirakawa abdicates in favor of Horikawa (in his eighth year), and carries on from retirement (beginning of *insei*, "rule by retired emperors").

Western Calendar Year	Japanese Calendar Year	Emperor	Regent, Shōgun, etc.	Events
1156	Hōgen 1	Go-shira-kawa	Fujiwara no Tadamichi, *Kanpaku*	Year of the Hōgen rebellion.
1159	Heiji 1	Nijō	Fujiwara no Motozane, *Kanpaku*	Heiji rebellion; death penalty reinstated.
1167	Nin'an 2	Rokujō	Fujiwara no Motofusa, *Sesshō*	Taira no Kiyomori made *Daijōdaijin*.
1180	Jishō 4	Antoku	Fujiwara no Motomichi, *Sesshō*	Minamoto no Yoritomo raises a military force, establishes headquarters at Kamakura; *samurai dokoro* established.
1184	Genryaku 1	Go-toba	Fujiwara no Motomichi, *Sesshō*	Yoritomo establishes the *kumonjo* and *monchūjo*.
1185	Bunji 1	Go-toba	Fujiwara no Motomichi, *Sesshō*	The Heike forces are destroyed; Senior Retired Emperor Goshirakawa issues a decree authorizing Yoritomo to hunt down his brother Yoshitsune; Ōe no Hiromoto advises Yoritomo to acquire the right to appoint *jitō* and *shugo*, and Hōjō Tokimasa goes to the capital for approval; the court appoints Yoritomo *sōtsuibushi* (general arresting officer) for the various provinces; Hōjō Tokimasa's petition that Yoritomo be made *sōjitō* (general land steward) and *sōshugo* (general military prepect) is granted.
1186	Bunji 2	Go-toba	Fujiwara no Kanezane, *Sesshō*	"Commissariat rice" (*hyōryōmai*) discontinued on Yoritomo's petition; *jitō* rights are abolished except for the lands vacated by those in rebellion.
1187	Bunji 3	Go-toba	Fujiwara no Kanezane, *Sesshō*	A recording office (*kirokusho*) for *shōen* established by the court.
1189	Bunji 5	Go-toba	Fujiwara no Kanezane, *Sesshō*	Yoritomo conquers Mutsu Province.
1190	Kenkyū 1	Go-toba	Fujiwara no Kanezane, *Sesshō*	Yoritomo goes to the capital, is appointed provisional grand councilor (*gon dainagon*) and general of inner palace guards, right division (*ukonoe no daishō*); Yoritomo resigns both these offices.
1192	Kenkyū 3	Go-toba	Minamoto no Yoritomo, *Sei-i-tai-shōgun*	Yoritomo appointed *Sei-i-tai-shōgun*.
1199	Shōji 1	Tsuchi-mikado	Minamoto no Yoriie, *Sei-i-tai-shōgun*	Yoritomo dies.
1221	Jōkyū 3	Chūkyō		Year of the Jōkyū rebellion, in which Kamakura forces defeat their enemies at court.

Western Calendar Year	Japanese Calendar Year	Emperor	Regent, Shōgun, etc.	Events
1223	Jōō 2	Go-hori-kawa		The portion of income due newly appointed *jitō* is fixed by the law of apportionment for new appointments (*shinpō rippō*).
1225	Karoku 1	Go-hori-kawa		Council of advisors (*hyojō shū*) established.
1232	Jōei 1	Shijō	Fujiwara no Yoritsune, *Sei-i-tai-shōgun*	*Goseibai Shikimoku* enacted.
1249	Kenchō 1	Go-fuka-kusa	Fujiwara no Yoritsugu, *Sei-i-tai-shōgun*	Hearing officers (*hikitsuke*) established, and appointments made to the board of hearing officers (*hikitsuke shū*).
1274	Bun'ei 11	Go-uda	Prince Ko-reyasu, *Sei-i-tai-shōgun*	First Mongol invasion.
1281	Kōan 4	Go-uda	Prince Ko-reyasu, *Sei-i-tai-shōgun*	Second Mongol invasion.
1294	Einin 2	Fushimi	Imperial Prince Hisa-akira, *Sei-i-tai-shōgun*	Kamakura *bakufu* discontinues all further consideration of rewards or punishments incidental to the second Mongol invasion.
1296	Einin 4	Fushimi	Imperial Prince Hisa-akira	Kyushu deputy (*chinzei tandai*) installed by Kamakura.
1297	Einin 5	Fushimi	Imperial Prince Takaakira	The *bakufu* issues a debt remission order (*tokusei rei*).
1317	Bunpō 1	Hanazono	Imperial Prince Mori-kuni, *Sei-i-tai-shōgun*	Rival lines of the imperial family agree, with encouragement of *bakufu*, that imperial succession should alternate between the two lines.
1333	Genkō 3	Go-daigo	Imperial Prince Morikuni, *Sei-i-tai-shōgun*	Kamakura *bakufu* destroyed; the new imperial government establishes a records office (*kirokusho*), a judicial office (*zasso ketsudanjo*), etc.
1338	Engen 3 Ryakuō 1	Komyō	Ashikaga Takauji, *Sei-i-tai-shōgun*	Ashikaga Takauji appointed *Sei-i-tai-shōgun*.
1352	Gan'ō 3	Go-mura-kami	Ashikaga Takauji, *Sei-i-tai-shōgun*	Takauji orders the expropriation of half the *shōen* proprietorship revenues (*hanzei hō*) in eight provinces requiring military action.
1368	Ōan 1	Go-kōgon	Ashikaga Yoshimitsu, *Sei-i-tai-shōgun*	*Hanzei hō* put into effect nationwide.
1392	Meitoku 3	Go-koma-tsu	Ashikaga Yoshimitsu *Sei-i-tai-shōgun*	Nothern and Southern courts reconciled.
1403	Ōei 10	Go-koma-tsu	Ashikaga Yoshimochi, *Sei-i-tai-shōgun*	Yoshimitsu sends an official message to the Ming, calling himself "King of Japan."

Western Calendar Year	Japanese Calendar Year	Emperor	Regent, Shōgun, etc.	Events
1441	Kakitsu 1	Go-hana-zono	Ashikaga Yoshinori, *Sei-i-tai-shōgun*	Debt remission (*tokusei rei*) ordered by *bakufu*.
1457	Chōroku 1	Go-hana-zono	Ashikaga Yoshimasa, *Sei-i-tai-shōgun*	Ōta Dōkan builds Edo castle.

EARLY MODERN PERIOD (*KINSEI*)

Western Calendar Year	Japanese Calendar Year	Emperor	Regent, Shōgun, etc.	Events
1467	Ōnin 1	Go-tsuchi-mikado	Ashikaga Yoshimasa, *Sei-i-tai-shōgun*	Outbreak of the Ōnin rebellion.
1526	Taiei 6	Go-nara	Ashikaga Yoshiharu, *Sei-i-tai-shōgun*	Imagawa Ujichika enacts the *kana mokuroku* as the law of his domain.
1536	Tenbun 5	Go-nara	Ashikaga Yoshiharu *Sei-i-tai-shōgun*	Date Tanemune enacts the *jinkaishū* as the law of his domain.
1547	Tenbun 16	Go-nara	Ashikaga Yoshiteru, *Sei-i-tai-shōgun*	Takeda Shingen enacts the "house laws of Shingen" (*Shingen kahō*) as the law of his domain.
1573	Tenshō 1	Ōgimachi	Ashikaga Yoshiaki, *Sei-i-tai-shōgun*	Muromachi *bakufu* destroyed.
1577	Tenshō 5	Ōgimachi	Nijō Haruyoshi, *Kanpaku*	Oda Nobunaga enacts rules for the town laid out below his main castle at Azuchi.
1582	Tenshō 10	Ōgimachi	Kujō Kaneta-ka, *Kanpaku*	Oda Nobunaga assassinated; Toyotomi Hideyoshi conducts a land survey of Yamishiro province (later expanded to a nation-wide survey).
1585	Tenshō 13	Ōgimachi	Toyotomi Hideyoshi, *Kanpaku*	Hideyoshi made *kanpaku*; selects five most trusted vassals and entrusts them with conduct of the government.
1587	Tenshō 15	Go-yōzei	Toyotomi Hideyoshi, *Kanpaku*	Hideyoshi conquers Kyushu; issues a prohibition against Christianity.
1588	Tenshō 16	Go-yōzei	Toyotomi, Hideyoshi *Kanpaku*	Hideyoshi issues "sword hunt" order, requring non-*samurai* to surrender their swords.
1590	Tenshō 18	Go-yōzei	Toyotomi Hideyoshi, *Kanpaku*	Hideyoshi conquers the Odawara (Hōjō), thereby completing the pacification of the empire; Tokugawa Ieyasu enters his new domain in the Kantō.
1591	Tenshō 19	Go-yōzei	Toyotomi Hideyoshi, *Kanpaku*	Hideyoshi prohibits *samurai* from becoming merchants or farmers.
1595	Bunroku 4	Go-yōzei	Toyotomi Hideyoshi, *Kanpaku*	Hideyoshi issues his "Osaka castle bulletin (*Osaka jōchū kabegaki*)" containing fundamental legal regulations for public affairs.
1598	Keichō 3	Go-yōzei	Toyotomi Hideyoshi	Five commissioners (*gobugyō*) appointed; Hideyoshi dies.

Western Calendar Year	Japanese Calendar Year	Emperor	Shōgun	Events
1600	Keichō 5	Go-yōzei	Kujō Kane-taka, *Kanpaku*	Battle of Sekigahara.
1603	Keichō 8	Go-yōzei	Tokugawa Ieyasu, *Sei-i-tai-shōgun*	Ieyasu becomes *Sei-i-tai-shōgun*.
1611	Keichō 16	Go-mizu-noo	Tokugawa Hidetada *Sei-i-tai-shōgun*	Written oaths of allegiance required of western *daimyō*.
1612	Keichō 17	Go-mizu-noo	Tokugawa Hidetada *Sei-i-tai-shōgun*	Written oaths of allegiance required of eastern *daimyō*.
1615	Genna 1 (Keichō 20)	Go-mizu-noo	Tokugawa Hidetada	Destruction of the Toyotomi house; laws for the warriors (*Buke sho-hatto*) enacted; laws for the palace and court nobility (*Kinchū narabini kuge sho-hatto*) enacted; "one province one castle" rule (*ikkoku ichijō no rei*) enacted, limiting each *daimyō* to one castle.
1632	Kan'ei 9	Empress Myōshō	Tokugawa Iemitsu	*Shoshi hatto* enacted, providing regulations for the (non-*daimyō*) vassals of the Tokugawa house.
1634	Kan'ei 11	Empress Myōshō	Tokugawa Iemitsu	Duties of senior councilors (*rōjū*) and junior councilors (*wakadoshiyori*) of *bakufu* defined.
1635	Kan'ei 12	Empress Myōshō	Tokugawa Iemitsu	Calls by foreign ships limited to Nagasaki; Iemitsu revises the *Buke sho-hatto* and institutes the system of "alternate attendance" (*sankin-kōtai*).
1637	Kan'ei 14	Empress Myōshō	Tokugawa Iemitsu	The Shimabara rebellion breaks out (to be suppressed in the following year).
1639	Kan'ei 16	Empress Myōshō	Tokugawa Iemitsu	Portuguese ships forbidden to land in Japan (completing the "closed country" policy).
1643	Kan'ei 20	Empress Myōshō	Tokugawa Iemitsu	Permanent sale of land by peasants forbidden.
1651	Keian 4	Go-kōmyō	Tokugawa Ietsuna	Adoption of a successor in expectation of death (*matsugo yōshi*) permitted [prohibition against this had caused several *daimyō* houses to become extinct, creating great numbers of masterless *samurai*, whose discontent had contributed to Yui Shōsetsu's rebellion earlier in the year].
1657	Meireki 3	Go-sai	Tokugawa Ietsuna	Great Meireki fire (in Edo).
1665	Kanbun 5	Reigen	Tokugawa Ietsuna	Tobacco growing on registered arable fields prohibited; official rulings (*osadame*) laid down for Buddhist temples of various sects; official rulings made for Shintō shrines in the provinces.
1673	Kanbun 13	Reigen	Tokugawa Ietsuna	Order issued limiting the division of land and prohibiting peasants from dividing

Western Calendar Year	Japanese Calendar Year	Emperor	Shōgun etc.	Events
				their arable lands into smaller parcels unless their total holdings are above a certain minimum putative yield in value.
1687	Jōkyō 4	Higashi-yama	Tokugawa Tsunayoshi	Orders requiring compassion for living beings issued by the *bakufu*.
1697	Genroku 10	Higashi-yama	Tokugawa Tsunayoshi	*Jibun shioki rei* enacted, recognizing the right of *daimyō* to exercise autonomous criminal justice powers (*jibun shioki*) over people in their fiefs.
1709	Hōei 6	Nakami-kado	Tokugawa Ienobu	Repeal of Tsunayoshi's penal laws forbidding cruelty to animals; Ienobu adopts the warrior laws (*Buke sho-hatto*) drafted by Arai Hakuseki.
1713	Shōtoku 3	Nakami-kado	Tokugawa Ietsugu	Prohibitions against land division (1673) amended, so as to impose a minimum quantity on lands to be separated from the main bloc, and on the remainder also.
1718	Kyōhō 3	Nakami-kado	Tokugawa Yoshimune	Neighborhood fire companies of townsmen (*machibikeshi*) organized in Edo.
1720	Kyōhō 5	Nakami-kado	Tokugawa Yoshimune	Tatooing instituted as a criminal punishment.
1721	Kyōhō 6	Nakami-kado	Tokugawa Yoshimune	A box for commoners' complaints against officials placed at the gate of the *hyōjosho* (judicial council) in Edo.
1722	Kyōhō 7	Nakami-kado	Tokugawa Yoshimune	Ōoka Echizen no Kami, *machi bugyō* (commissioner of the townspeople), organizes Edo neighborhood chiefs into leagues; *bakufu* imposes a 1-percent rice assessment (*agemai*) on the putative incomes of the *daimyō*, while relaxing "alternate attendance" requirements; finance commissioners (*kanjō bugyō*) are divided into administrative officers (*okattemuki goyōkata*) and judicial officers (*kujikata*); tax imposts on Edo neighborhoods levied in silver (rather than goods or services).
1723	Kyōhō 8	Nakami-kado	Tokugawa Yoshimune	*Bakufu* institutes a system of supplementary office stipends (*tashidaka*) to encourage talented but low-ranking *samurai*, whose hereditary stipends were also low, to aspire to high office. Under the rule, if an office was awarded to one of lower rank than was usually the case, his stipend would be raised to the appropriate level for so long as he held the office.
1736	Genbun 1	Sakura-machi	Tokugawa Yoshimune	*Bakufu* limits recoverable interest to 15 percent per year.
1737	Genbun 2	Sakura-machi	Tokugawa Yoshimune	Bakufu rules that land transferred as security for a loan can be redeemed only within ten years after the term of the mortgage agreement expires.

Western Calendar Year	Japanese Calendar Year	Emperor	Shōgun	Events
1742	Kanpō 2	Sakura-machi	Tokugawa Yoshimune	*Kujikata Osadamegaki* enacted.
1759	Hōreki 9	Momozono	Tokugawa Ieshige	Restrictions against land division imposed during Yoshimune's shogunate repealed; rule of 1713 restored.
1789	Kansei 1	Kōkaku	Tokugawa Ienari	Abrogation order (*kien rei*) cancels all debts to rice brokers incurred by *bakufu* housemen and bannermen within the preceding six years.
1790	Kansei 2	Kōkaku	Tokugawa Ienari	"Labor rehabilitation center" (*ninsoku yoseba*) established.
1805	Bunka 2	Kōkaku	Tokugawa Ienari	The *bakufu* establishes a regional police administration for the eight Kantō provinces.
1825	Bunsei 8	Ninkō	Tokugawa Ienari	*Bakufu* orders that foreign ships be repulsed.
1841	Tenpō 12	Ninkō	Tokugawa Ieyoshi	"Tenpō reforms" begin; wholesalers' trade associations (*tonya kabunakama*) disbanded by *bakufu*.
1842	Tenpō 13	Ninkō	Tokugawa Ieyoshi	Order of 1825 to repulse foreign ships relaxed.
1843	Tenpō 14	Ninkō	Tokugawa Ieyoshi	Chief councilor Mizuno Tadakuni issues an order bringing all lands within ten *ri* (about 24 miles) of Edo and 5 *ri* of Osaka within direct bakufu control, but the order is withdrawn within a month's time.
1851	Kaei 4	Kōmei	Tokugawa Ieyoshi	Wholesalers' associations reinstated.
1853	Kaei 6	Kōmei	Tokugawa Ieyoshi	Perry's ships arrive at Uraga; the *bakufu* informs the *daimyō* about the American message and requests their opinions; injunction against building large ships withdrawn.
1854	Ansei 1	Kōmei	Tokugawa Iesada	Treaty of friendship with the United States.
1858	Ansei 5	Kōmei	Tokugawa Iesada	The *bakufu*'s request to the imperial court to conclude a commercial treaty with the United States is denied; the *bakufu* concludes a commercial treaty with the United States.

MODERN PERIOD (KINDAI)

Western Calendar Year	Japanese Calendar Year	Emperor	Shōgun	Events
1862	Bunkyū 2	Kōmei	Tokugawa Iemochi	The *bakufu* relaxes the rules of alternate attendance (*sankin-kōtai*).
1863	Bunkyū 3	Kōmei	Tokugawa Iemochi	*Shōgun* Iemochi petitions the court that he be entrusted with affairs of state in accordance with established practice, but the court answers that in state affairs it will consult directly with the various fiefs as circumstances dictate.

Western Calendar Year	Japanese Calendar Year	Emperor	Chief Minister	Events
1864	Genji 1	Kōmei	Tokugawa Iemochi	First expedition against Chōshū.
1865	Keiō 1	Kōmei	Tokugawa Iemochi	Treaties confirmed by imperial edict.
1866	Keiō 2	Kōmei	Tokugawa Iemochi	Second expedition against Chōshū; agreement on tariffs concluded with the United States, Britain, France, and the Netherlands.
1867	Keiō 3	Meiji	Tokugawa Yoshinobu (Keiki)	Hyōgo (modern Kobe) opened to foreign commerce; the court issues a secret edict authorizing the overthrow of the *bakufu*; the *bakufu* returns sovereign power to the emperor; Yoshinobu announces his resignation as *shōgun*; the court proclaims its resumption of its ancient sovereign powers (*ōsei fukko*).
1868	Meiji 1	Meiji	Arisugawa no miya, Imperial Prince Taruhito, Chief Executive (*Sōsai*)	Battles of Toba and Fushimi; five-article Charter Oath; *Seitaisho* issued; Edo renamed Tokyo; era name changed to"Meiji", with the intention to make all era names in the future correspond to imperial reigns; validation of each village's area and of peasant land ownership.
1869	Meiji 2	Meiji	Sanjō Sanetomi, *Udaijin*	The *daimyō* of Satsuma, Chōshū, Tosa, and Hizen announce their surrender of control over land and people in their domains to the imperial government; *kōgisho* (deliberative assembly) opened; the emperor moves to Tokyo; *daimyō* made to return their powers over their domains to the emperor; court nobles (*kuge*) and *daimyō* families given new official status as peers (*kazoku*); civil service code (*Shokuin Rei*) enacted; system of domain government officials established, making most *daimyō* governors of their old fiefs.
1870	Meiji 3	Meiji	Sanjō Sanetomi, *Udaijin*	*Shūgiin* (former *kōgisho*) opened; commoners permitted to have surnames; the new criminal law (*Shinritsu Kōryō*) promulgated; common people forbidden to wear swords; former *samurai* diveded into *shizoku* and *sotsu*.
1871	Meiji 4	Meiji	Sanjō Sanetomi, *Dajōdaijin*	Domains of shrines and temples confiscated; household registration law promulgated; Ministry of Justice (*shihōshō*) established; reorganization of the *dajōkan* (into the three divisions of *sei-in*, *sa-in*, and *u-in*); sword-wearing made optional for former *samurai*; *eta* and *hinin* abolished as official class designations; landowners permitted to cultivate whatever they wish; title certificates issued for land in the Tokyo capital district.

Western Calendar Year	Japanese Calendar Year	Emperor	Chief Minister	Events
1872	Meiji 5	Meiji	Sanjō Sane-tomi, *Dajō-daijin*	Publication of regulations governing issuance of land and collection of revenue; status of *sotsu* abolished; abrogation of the ban prohibiting the permanent sale of land enacted; regulations governing the delivery of land titles in land sales and transfers enacted; Ministry of War (*Hyō-bushō*) replaced by the ministries of the army and the navy; government decides to grant title certificates to all those having possession (*shoji*) of land; public educational system begun; order liberating indentured *geisha* and prostitutes promulgated; Gregorian calendar adopted; proclamation of imperial edict announcing military conscription.
1873	Meiji 6	Meiji	Sanjō Sane-tomi, *Dajōdaijin*	Conscription order promulgated; taking of revenge strictly forbidden, but later allowed under certain circumstances; Japanese permitted to marry foreigners; *dajōkan* system revised; wives allowed to sue husbands for divorce; Amended Criminal Code enacted; land tax reform regulations promulgated; Ministry of Home Affairs (*Naimusho*) established; regulations for the commutation of warrior stipends enacted; arrival of Boissonade in Japan.
1874	Meiji 7	Meiji	Sanjō Sane-tomi, *Dajōdaijin*	Memorial for the creation of a popularly elected assembly presented to the *sa-in;* Tokyo Metropolitan Police Office established; Fundamental Rules for National Assembly (*Giin Kenpō*) promulgated; judges permitted to reduce sentences of convicted criminals where warranted by extenuating circumstances.
1875	Meiji 8	Meiji	Sanjō Sane-tomi, *Dajōdaijin*	Society of Patriots (*Aikokusha*) organized at Osaka conference of the political opposition movement; commoners legally required to assume surnames; civil litigation hearings opened to the general public; imperial edict proclaims the eventual establishment of constitutional government, and announces the abolition of the *sa-in* and *u-in* and the establishment of a legislative senate (*genrōin*). A supreme court (*daishin'in*) and assemblies of local governors (*chihōkan kaigi*) founded; libel law and newspaper regulations enacted. Assembly of local governors opened; preliminary interrogation of criminal suspects by examining judges instituted; marriages, adoptions, affiliations, divorces, or disownments ruled invalid unless entered in household registers.

Western Calendar Year	Japanese Calendar Year	Emperor	Chief Minister	Events
1876	Meiji 9	Meiji	Sanjō Sanetomi, Dajōdaijin	Control and punishment of prostitution delegated to metropolitan police and local administrators; Regulations for Attorneys issued; Sword Ban Order issued, prohibiting sword-wearing except for officials or state ceremonies; criminal convictions henceforth required to be based on proof (rather than confessions exclusively); Regulations for the Issuance of Pension Bonds issued, providing for the compulsory conversion of all *samurai* stipends into government bonds. *Genrōin* receives an imperial rescript ordering that a national constitution be drafted; rebellion against land tax reforms in Ibaraki Prefecture.
1877	Meiji 10	Meiji	Sanjō Sanetomi, Dajōdaijin	Land tax rate lowered by imperial decree; outbreak of Satsuma rebellion; issuance of bail regulations.
1878	Meiji 11	Meiji	Sanjō Sanetomi, Dajōdaijin	Final half of a draft civil code completed; promulgation of the Law Governing the Organization of Rural Districts, City Wards, Towns and Villages; prefectural assembly regulations and local tax regulations issued; initiation and pursuit of criminal prosecution made the exclusive function of procurators; General Staff Office established.
1879	Meiji 12	Meiji	Sanjō Sanetomi, Dajōdaijin	Education Order enacted, prescribing rules for organization of schools and compulsory education; repeal of all legal rules relating to torture.
1880	Meiji 13	Meiji	Sanjō Sanetomi, Dajōdaijin	Board of Audit established; the Society of Patriots (*Aikokusha*) renamed the League for Establishing a National Assembly (*Kokkai Kisei Dōmei*); Regulations for Public Meetings restrict political gatherings; City Ward, Town and Village Assembly Law promulgated; Old Criminal Code and Code of Criminal Instruction enacted (but not put into effect until 1882); Regulations on the Transfer of Factories to Private Control enacted.
1881	Meiji 14	Meiji	Sanjō Sanetomi, Dajodaijin	Iwakura Tomomi produces his General Principles for a Constitution (*Kenpō Kōryō*); Hokkaido land scandal occurs; Imperial Announcement of the Establishment of a National Assembly in the Twenty-Third Year of Meiji.
1882	Meiji 15	Meiji	Sanjō Sanetomi, Dajōdaijin	Itō Hirobumi departs for Europe for the investigation of constitutional law; Bank of Japan Regulations and Martial Law Order enacted.
1883	Meiji 16	Meiji	Sanjo Sanetomi, Dajōdaijin	Itō Hirobumi returns to Japan.

Western Calendar Year	Japanese Calendar Year	Emperor	Prime Minister	Events
1884	Meiji 17	Meiji	Sanjō Sane-tomi, *Dajōdaijin*	General Regulations for Mediation (*Kankai Ryakusoku*), for official settlement of suits, published by Ministry of Justice; enactment of the Ordinance Concerning Peers, establishing five ranks of nobility.
1885	Meiji 18	Meiji	Itō Hirobumi, Prime Minister	Enactment of Summary Trial Regulations for Police Offenses (*Ikeizai Sokketsu Rei*); *dajōkan* system abolished and replaced by cabinet system.
1886	Meiji 19	Meiji	Itō Hirobumi	Promulgation of Formalities for Official Documents (*Kōbunshiki*), distinguishing between statute law (which, after a diet was organized, would require its approval) and ordinance; promulgation of General Rules for the Organization of the Various Ministries; Order for an Imperial University established Tokyo University as the central government academy; Regulations Governing the Organization of the Courts issued; promulgation of Registration Law, providing for public recording of property interests in ships, land, or buildings.
1887	Meiji 20	Meiji	Itō Hirobumi	Income Tax Law enacted; Peace Preservation Regulations (*Hoan Jōrei*) enacted, limiting political demonstrations and gatherings and permitting banishment of opposition leaders from Tokyo.
1888	Meiji 21	Meiji	Kuroda Kiyotaka	Enactment of Regulations Governing the Organization of Cities and Regulations Governing the Organization of Towns and Villages (put into effect during 1889 and 1890); Regulations Governing the Organization of the Privy Council are issued, and the new Privy Council holds a conference on the proposed Constitution.
1889	Meiji 22	Meiji	Yamagata Aritomo	Promulgation of the Constitution, the Law of the House of Representatives, the Law of Election of Members of the House of Representatives, the Imperial Ordinance Concerning the House of Peers, and the Law of Finance; Imperial House Law enacted; publication of the "Statement of Views on the Compilation of the Law Codes" by the Jurists' Society; Regulations Governing Cabinet Organization enacted.
1890	Meiji 23	Meiji	Yamagata Aritomo	Promulgation of Law of the Constitution of the Courts (put into effect, 1891); enactment of Civil Code ("Old Civil Code," with chapters on property, acquisition of property, security interest, and evidence), scheduled for enforcement in 1893, and Code of Civil Procedure (put into force in 1891); promulgation of Commercial Code ("Old Commercial Code"), to

Western Calendar Year	Japanese Calendar Year	Emperor	Prime Minister	Events
				take effect in 1891; promulgation of Regulations Governing the Organization of Prefectures and Regulations Governing the Organization of Rural Districts (neither to go immediately into effect), and of the Public Meeting and Political Party Law; Code of Criminal Instruction repealed, and Code of Criminal Procedure promulgated; first Imperial Diet opens.
1891	Meiji 24	Meiji	Matsukata Masayoshi	Promulgation of remaining portions of the Civil Code (additional provisions of the chapter on acquisition of property and a chapter on the law of persons). Otsu Incident demonstrates independence of judiciary.
1892	Meiji 25	Meiji	Itō Hirobumi	Dispute over enforcement of the new codes reaches a crescendo; enforcement of the civil and commercial codes postponed until 1896.
1893	Meiji 26	Meiji	Itō Hirobumi	Promulgation of the Lawyer's Law; Rules for the Codes Investigation Committee determined, and the committee begins examining civil and commercial codes; certain sections of the Commercial Code allowed to go into effect; office of Chief of the Naval Central Staff established.
1894	Meiji 27	Meiji	Itō Hirobumi	Conclusion of a revised commercial treaty with Great Britain.
1896	Meiji 29	Meiji	Matsukata Masayoshi	First three chapters of the New Civil Code promulgated (put into effect, 1898); enforcement of civil and commercial codes further postponed.
1898	Meiji 31	Meiji	Itō Hirobumi; Okuma Shigenobu; Yamagata Aritomo	Formation of Okuma-Itagaki cabinet; final two chapters of New Civil Code promulgated; the entire New Civil Code goes into effect.
1899	Meiji 32	Meiji	Yamagata Aritomo	Old Commercial Code repealed (except for Chapter 3 on bankruptcy) and New Commercial Code promulgated.
1900	Meiji 33	Meiji	Itō Hirobumi	Imperial ordinance requires that military cabinet ministers be general officers on active duty.
1905	Meiji 38	Meiji	Katsura Tarō	Enactment of laws on the deferral of execution of criminal punishments.
1906	Meiji 39	Meiji	Saionji Kinmochi	Enactment of Law for the Nationalization of Railways.
1907	Meiji 40	Meiji	Saionji Kinmochi	Law Concerning Forms of Promulgation (Kōshiki Rei) goes into effect, repealing 1886 Formalities for Official Documents; enactment of the New Criminal Code set for October 1908.

Western Calendar Year	Japanese Calendar Year	Emperor	Prime Minister	Events
1908	Meiji 41	Meiji	Katsura Tarō	An Inspector General of Education established in the army.
1909	Meiji 42	Meiji	Katsura Tarō	Enactment of the Law concerning the Protection of Buildings.
1911	Meiji 44	Meiji	Saionji Kinmochi	Enactment of Factory Law (enforced in 1916); restoration of tariff autonomy.
1913	Taishō 2	Taishō	Yamamoto Gonnohyōe	Repeal of the rule requiring army and navy ministers to be officers on active duty.
1914	Taishō 3	Taishō	Ōkuma Shigenobu	Amendment of Household Registration Law (abolishing the "status register" recording ancestry, etc); supreme court establishes rule protecting unregistered (naien) marriages by treating them as actionable promises to marry.
1916	Taishō 5	Taishō	Terauchi Masataka	Factory Law put into effect.
1918	Taishō 7	Taishō	Hara Satoshi	Enactment of the Law for the Mobilization of Strategic Industries.
1921	Taishō 10	Taishō	Takahashi Korekiyo	Enactment of Law Concerning the Abolition of the System of Rural Districts (depriving the gun of status as governing bodies, enforced in 1923).
1922	Taishō 11	Taishō	Katō Tomosaburō	Enactment of Juvenile Law, establishing juvenile courts, and the Law of Reformatories (both enforced in 1923); enactment of the new Code of Criminal Procedure (enforced in 1924).
1923	Taishō 12	Taishō	Yamamoto Gonnohyōe	Enactment of the Jury Law (put into effect in 1928), allowing fact-finding by juries in certain criminal cases.
1924	Taishō 13	Taishō	Kiyoura Keigo; Katō Takaaki	Law for the Conciliation of Agricultural Tenancy Disputes enacted.
1925	Taishō 14	Taishō	Katō Takaaki	Law on Landing of Foreign Persons enacted; Universal Male Suffrage Law enacted.
1926	Taishō 15	Taishō	Wakatsuki Reijirō	Law for the Conciliation of Labor Disputes enacted; a new Code of Civil Procedure enacted (enforced in 1929); judicial decision imposes the duty of chastity on the husband as well as the wife.
1927	Shōwa 2	Present Emperor	Tanaka Giichi	Enactment of Military Service Law, replacing the Conscription Order of 1873.
1928	Shōwa 3	Present Emperor	Tanaka Giichi	First general election under the Universal Male Suffrage Law.
1929	Shōwa 4	Present Emperor	Hamaguchi Osachi	Enactment of Juvenile Correction Law.
1931	Shōwa 6	Present Emperor	Wakatsuki Reijirō; Inukai Tsuyoshi	Law for the Control of Essential Industries enacted; Law for Relief to Accidentally Injured Laborers enacted; enactment of Law for Compensation for Criminally

Western Calendar Year	Japanese Calendar Year	Emperor	Prime Minister	Events
				Convicted, establishing a system of damages for those mistakenly convicted; enactment of Rules for Investigating Cases of Conditional Release of Prisoners; Manchurian Incident takes place in China.
1932	Shōwa 7	Present Emperor	Saitō Makoto	May 15th Incident, the murder of Prime Minister Inukai by military personnel; Inukai cabinet (the last party cabinet under the Meiji Constitution) falls.
1933	Shōwa 8	Present Emperor	Saitō Makoto	Japan announces its withdrawal from the League of Nations.
1934	Shōwa 9	Present Emperor	Okada Keisuke	Japan announces its repudiation of the Washington treaties.
1935	Shōwa 10	Present Emperor	Okada Keisuke	Controversy breaks out over the "organ theory" of the emperor's role.
1936	Shōwa 11	Present Emperor	Hirota Kōki	Repudiation of the London Naval Disarmament Treaty; February 26th Incident occurs; rule requiring army and navy ministers to be officers on active duty reinstated; mutual defense pact concluded with Germany.
1937	Shōwa 12	Present Emperor	Hayashi Senjūrō; Konoe Fumimaro	Italy included in mutual defense pact with Germany.
1938	Shōwa 13	Present Emperor	Konoe Fumimaro	National General Mobilization Act enacted.
1939	Shōwa 14	Present Emperor	Hiranuma Kiichirō; Abe Nobuyuki	Promulgation of Labor Conscription Order and Price Control Order.
1940	Shōwa 15	Present Emperor	Yonai Mitsumasa; Konoe Fumimaro	Senior Statesmen Conference convened to select the prime minister and cabinet; Imperial Rule Assistance Association organized.
1941	Showa 16	Present Emperor	Konoe Fumimaro; Tōjō Hideki	Outbreak of the Pacific War.
1942	Shōwa 17	Present Emperor	Tōjō Hideki	Enactment of Control of Foodstuffs Law.
1943	Shōwa 18	Present Emperor	Tōjō Hideki	Restrictions placed on the deliberating powers of city, town, and village assemblies; power of the prime minister strengthened; operation of Jury Law suspended.
1944	Shōwa 19	Present Emperor	Koiso Kuniaki	
1945	Showa 20	Present Emperor	Suzuki Kantarō; Prince Higashikuni;	July—Potsdam Declaration August—Soviet declaration of war against Japan; acceptance of Potsdam Declaration

Western Calendar Year	Japanese Calendar Year	Emperor	Prime Minister	Events

CONTEMPORARY PERIOD (GENDAI)

| | | | Shidehara Kijūrō | September—Document of Surrender signed; Potsdam Declaration accepted, and State of Emergency Edict put into effect; directive removing restrictions on freedom of speech and of the press (the simple term "directive" as used here always refers to directives of the Supreme Commander for the Allied Powers [SCAP]). October—Memorandum demanding the removal of restrictions on political, civil, or religious liberties (a directive requiring the repeal of the Peace Preservation Law and National Defense Security Law, the immediate release of political prisoners, the dissolution of the Special Higher Police and freedom to criticize the emperor system); repeal of the Peace Preservation Law and National Defense Security Laws; SCAP suggests five major reforms, equal rights for both sexes, encouragement of labor unions, liberalization of education, emancipation from despotic government, and democratization of the economic system; abolition of the General Staff and the Naval Command; directives outline general policies for the educational system and require that militaristic educational personnel be purged. November—Directive ordering *zaibatsu* holdings frozen and dispersed; directive freezing assets of the Imperial Household; directive ordering the arrest of suspected war criminals. December—Directive ordering agricultural land reform; directive ordering the separation of Shintō from the state; new election law enacted; SCAP announces that the basic directive for democratization of Japan is accomplished; enactment of the Labor Union Law (put into effect March 1946); directive prohibiting education in moral training, Japanese history, and geography. |
| 1946 | Shōwa 21 | Present Emperor | Yoshida Shigeru | January—The emperor issues an edict denying his divinity; directive ordering purge of all militarists from public office and the dissolution of all ultranationalistic organizations. February—First execution of land reform policy; the government submits a Draft Constitution to SCAP; SCAP delivers the MacArthur Draft Constitution to the Japanese government; directive for dealing with the currency crisis (freezing bank savings); Ordinance for Dismissal of Public Officials promulgated. March—The government publishes the Outline Draft for |

Western Calendar Year	Japanese Calendar Year	Emperor	Prime Minister	Events
				Constitutional Revision. April—General elections held for the Lower House under the new election law; the government publishes the complete text of the new Constitution. May—International Military Tribunal for the Far East opens. September—Protection of Livelihood Law and Labor Relations Adjustment Law enacted. October—Enactment of the Special Measures for the Creation of Owner-farmers. November—Promulgation of the Constitution of Japan.
1947	Shōwa 22	Present Emperor	Katayama Tetsu	January—The Ordinance for the Dismissal of Public Officials is revised (extending it to the areas of finance and the media, and to local officials). April—Enactment of the Basic Law of Education and the School Education Law; enactment of the Labor Standards Law; enactment of the Antimonopoly Law; enactment of the Administrative Offices Law, the Local Autonomy Law, the Diet Law, and the Courts Law; enactment of Law concerning Emergency Measures of Civil Law Accompanying the Enforcement of the Constitution of Japan. May—Enforcement of the Constitution of Japan. July—Organization of the Fair Trade Commission (the regulatory agency created by the Antimonopoly Law). October—Enactment of the National Public Service Law. December—Enactment of the Law for the Elimination of Excessive Concentrations of Economic Power.
1948	Shōwa 23	Present Emperor	Ashida Hitoshi	January—Enforcement of the Amended Civil Code and the new Household Registration Law. March—Enforcement of the Police Law. April—Enforcement of the Child Welfare Law. July—Enactment of the Boards of Education Law (providing for administration by local boards), the Code of Criminal Procedure, the Law concerning Policemen's Performance of Their Duties, the Habeas Corpus Law, and the Organization of National Administrative Agencies Law. November—The International Military Tribunal for the Far East renders judgment; National Public Employees Law revised (so as to prohibit strikes, etc.).

Western Calendar Year	Japanese Calendar Year	Emperor	Prime Minister	Events
1949	Shōwa 24	Present Emperor	Yoshida Shigeru	January—Code of Criminal Procedure put into effect; Family Courts put into operation. March—Order for the Regulation of Associations promulgated (by the occupation to control anti-democratic organizations). May—Unemployment Insurance Law enacted; enactment of Law Prescribing the Numbers of Public Employees. September—Civil Service Commission regulations limit political activities by public employees.
1950	Shōwa 29	Present Emperor	Yoshida Shigeru	January—Enactment of Criminal Compensation Law (for reimbursement of persons wrongfully convicted or imprisoned). April—Enactment of Election of Public Officials Law. June—Outbreak of the Korean War. July—MacArthur orders the organization of the National Police Reserve. August—(Cabinet) directive establishing the National Police Reserve. October—SCAP permits wide-scale depurging of persons barred from public life. December—Local Public Employees Law (prohibiting strikes, etc.) enacted.
1951	Shōwa 26	Present Emperor	Yoshida Shigeru	March—Enactment of the Social Welfare Services Law. June—Amendment of the Police Law. July—The government announces the completion of the breakup of *zaibatsu* holdings. September—Peace Treaty with the United States concluded; Japan-U.S. Security Treaty concluded.

BIBLIOGRAPHY

I. General Reference

Readers who may wish to pursue the present subject in greater depth are directed, first, to the detailed bibliography in Ishii Ryō-suke, *Nihon hōseishi gaiyō* [A Concise History of Japanese Law] (Tokyo : Sōbunsha, 1952), which includes publication up to 1950. Materials for 1945–1959 can be found in *Hōseishi bunken mokuroku Shōwa 20 – Showa 34* [Bibliography of Legal History 1945–1959] (Sōbunsha, 1962), edited by the Nihon Hōseishi Gakkai (Japan Legal History Association). This Association has also been editing, at the rate of one volume a year, a journal entitled *Hōseishi Kenkyū* [Studies in Legal History] (Sōbunsha), which includes a comprehensive descriptive bibliography covering the publications of the preceding year. In commemoration of its twentieth anniversary, in 1971, the Association also published a special issue, *Hōseishi gakkai kaiin bunken mokuroku* [Bibliographies for Members of the Japan Legal History Association] (Sōbunsha, 1971), which covers developments from 1960 to 1969.

English bibliographies in the field include the following: Ishii Ryōsuke. *Bibliographical Introduction to Legal History and Ethnology*, *E/13*: *Japan* (l'Institut de Sociologie, Université Libre de Bru-xelles, 1964); and Kokusai Bunka Shinkōkai, ed., *K.B.S. Biblio-graphy of Standard Reference Books for Japanese Studies with Descriptive Notes*, vol. IX-B: *Law, Parts I* (1968) and *II* (1970).

155

II. General Explanatory Works

Takigawa Masajirō, *Nihon hōseishi* (Legal History of Japan). Tokyo: Yūhikaku, 1923.

A survey of the field from the archaic period to the Edo era. The author's special subject is *ritsuryō*, on which the treatment is excellent. The method of historical division here reflects the originality of the author's view, as compared to the conventional treatments usual abroad: the period of Native Japanese Law (Law of Clans), the period of adopted Chinese Law (*Ritsuryō*), and the period of Assimilation (Warrior Law).

Maki Kenji. *Nihon hōseishi gairon* (Outline of Japanese Legal History) Complete ed. Tokyo: Kōbundō, 1948.

A survey from the achaic period to the end of Edo. To the complete edition of 1948 was added a survey on developments since the Meiji Restoration. The author's specialty is the feudal system in the Kamakura era; this work, however, is written with materials in a well-balanced arrangement so as to bring forth the author's view of the characteristics of each period.

Takayanagi Shinzō. *Nihon hōseishi* (Legal History of Japan) I & II. Tokyo: Yūhikaku, 1949, 1965.

A concise outline. The first volume covers the archaic period to the Edo era, and the second the Meiji Restoration to the period of Modern State Law. The author presents significant problems of Japanese legal history arising from the process by which traditional Japanese elements and elements of external origin were combined and amalgamated in various forms.

Ishii Ryōsuke. *Nihon hōseishi gaisetsu* (An Outline History of Japanese Law). Tokyo: Kōbundō, 1948. Reprint edition: Sōbunsha, 1960.

A voluminous general legal history, written wth a unique periodization called *hadō-shikan* (fluctuating view of history). According to the author, the history of his subject is divided into four stages before the end of the Edo era: *Jōdai* (Archaic Age), *Jōsei* (Ancient Age), *Chūsei* (Middle Ages) and *Kinsei* (Early Modern Age). The detailed index at the end also makes this publication useful as a compact dictionary.

Ishii Ryōsuke. *Nihon hōseishi gaiyō* (A Concise History of Japanese Law). Tokyo: Sōbunsha, 1952.

Written as a textbook for students in the Faculty of Law of the University of Tokyo. The author has compressed and simplified his earlier book, *Nihon hōseishi gaisetsu,* and added a survey of modern law in and after the Meiji era.

Ishii Ryōsuke. *Hōseishi: Taikei Nihonshi sōsho* (Series of Systematic Japanese History). Vol. IV. Tokyo: Yamakawa, 1964.
The entire history of Japan, from the archaic period to the present day, from the viewpoint of the development of public law. The author pursues his *hadō-shikan* (fluctuating view of history) as in the above two publications, here with emphasis on political structure and the *shōen* (manor) system.

Ishii Ryōsuke. *Tennō: Tennō tōchi no shiteki kaimei* (The Emperor: An Historical Explanation of Sovereignty). Tokyo: Kōbundō, 1950.
The author argues that there was no tradition of direct administration by the emperor in Japanese history, except for brief periods when the imperial institution took on such an appearance under the influence of Chinese or Prussian legal systems.

Ishii Ryōsuke. *Keibatsu no rekishi* (History of Punishment), in *Hōritsugaku taikei* (Series on Jurisprudence). Part 2, *Hōgaku riron hen* (Legal Theory) Vol. 134–B. Tokyo: Nihon Hyōronsha, 1952.
The author considers that forms of punishment should be studied as a part of the history of punitive law, and has arranged the history of punishment in Japan into five periods; the Archaic, Ancient, Middle, Early Modern, and Late Modern periods.

Takigawa Masajirō. *Nihon gyōseishi* (History of Penology). Tokyo: Seiabō, 1961.
Consists of sixteen essays divided into two parts: the history of penology and the history of the prison system.

Kobayakawa Kingo. *Nihon tanpohōshi josetsu* (Introduction to the History of Japanese Security Law). Osaka: Hōbunkan, 1933.
The institutional history of material and personal security as credit security from the time of *Ritsuryō* system to the Edo era.

Ishii Ryōsuke. *Chōshi sōzokusei* (The System of Primogeniture) in *Hōritsugaku taikei* (Series on Jurisprudence). Part 2, *Hōgaku riron hen* (Legal Theory). Vol. 84. Nihon Hyōronsha, 1950.

The author touches in the introduction on the Hebraic, Indian, Greek, French, British and German systems, and expands his argument to the development of primogeniture in Japan from the Archaic Period to the Early Modern.

III. Collected Articles

Miura Hiroyuki. *Hōseishi no kenkyū* (Studies in Legal History). 1919. Reprint: Tokyo: Iwanami Shoten, 1973.
— —. *Zoku hōseishi no kenkyū* (Further Studies in Legal History), 1925. Reprint: Iwanami Shoten, 1973.
A selection of sixty-nine articles on legal history from the archaic period to the end of Edo. The author, who has taught medieval Japanese history (Faculty of Literature) and legal history (Faculty of Law) at Kyoto University, is known as the advocate of "humanistic legal history."

Nakada Kaoru. *Hōseishi ronshū* (Collected Essays on Legal History). Tokyo: Iwanami Shoten.
Vol.   I *Shinzokuhō sōzōkuhō* (Family Law and Law of Succession), 1926. Reprint 1970.
Vol. II *Bukkenhō* (Law of *jus in rem*), 1938. Reprint 1970.
Vol. III *Saikenhō oyobi zat'cho* (Credit Law etc.), 1943. Reprint 1971.
Vol. IV *Hoi* (Miscellaneous), 1964. Reprint 1971.
A selection of eighty-eight articles by the "founder of Japanese legal history." The author's achievement lies in having established a system in the study of ancient law based on the principles and ideas of legal science, and in his firm grasp of their characteristics. Also, through his knowledge of comparative law he has incorporated Japan's ancient law into the framework of world legal history.

Nakada Kaoru (ed.). *Miyazaki sensei hōseishi ronshū* (Professor Miyazaki's Collected Studies on Legal History). Tokyo: Iwanami Shoten, 1929.
The first part of this book compares Japanese and Chinese legal systems, and the second compares the Japanese and Korean languages in an attempt to apply comparative studies of Oriental languages to the study of Japanese legal history.

Takigawa Masajirō. *Nihon hōseishi kenkyū* (Studies in Japanese

Legal History). Tokyo: Yūhikaku. 1941.

A collection of 30 essays. The author subsequently compiled his research into four volumes titled *Hōseishi ronsō* (Essays on Legal History), (Tokyo: Kadokawa Shoten : 1967), divided as follows:

Ritsuryō kyakushiki no kenkyū (Studies of Ritsuryō and Kyakushiki).

Kyōsei narabini tojōsei no kenkyū (Studies of Capital Systems and Rules for Capitals).

Ritsuryō renmin-sei no kenkyū (Studies of Slavery in the Ritsuryō System).

Ritsuryō shosei oyobi ryōge no kan no kenkyū (Studies of Institutions under the Ritsuryō Government and Extra-legal Officials).

In these volumes, the author gives full expression to his constant assertion that "legal history is the history of legal life."

IV. Jōdai, Jōsei

Sakima Kōei. *Nyonin seiji-kō* (Women's Thought on Politics). Tokyo: Oka Shoin, 1926.

Ishii Ryōsuke & Inoue Mitsusada. *Shinpojiumu Yamataikoku* (Symposium Yamataikoku). Tokyo: Sōbunsha, 1961.

Inoue, Mitsusada. *Nihon kokka no kigen* (Origin of the Japanese State). Tokyo: Iwanami Shoten, 1960.

Ishio Yoshihisa. *Nihon kodaihō no kenkyū* (A Study of Ancient Japanese Law). Tokyo: Hōritsu Bunkasha, 1959.

Sakamoto Tarō. *Taika no kaishin no kenkyū* (Study of the Taika Reform). Tokyo: Shibundō, 1938.

Ishii Ryōsuke. *Taika no kaishin to Kamakura bakufu no seiritsu* (The Taika Reform and the Formation of the Kamakura Bakufu). Tokyo: Sōbunsha, 1958.

Takigawa Masajirō. *Ritsuryō no kenkyū* (Studies of the Ritsuryō), 1931. Reprint: Tokyo: Tōkō Shoin, 1966.

Takigawa Masajirō. *Hōseishi-jō yori mitaru Nihon nōmin no seikatsu* (Life of Japanese Farmers as Seen from Legal History), 2 vols. Tokyo: Tōkō Shoin, 1940.

Imamiya Shin. *Handen shūju-sei no kenkyū* (Study of the Handen Allotment System). Tokyo: Ryūginsha, 1944.

Sakamoto Tarō. *Jōdai ekisei no kenkyū* (Study of the Posting Station System in Ancient Japan). Tokyo: Shibundō, 1928.

Rikō Mitsuo. *Saiban no rekishi* (A History of the Trial). *Nihon rekishi shinsho* (New Series of Japanese History) 3. Tokyo: Shibundō, 1964.

V. Chūsei

Ueki Naoichirō. *Goseibai shikimoku no kenkyū* (Study of *Goseibai Shikimoku*), Tokyo: Iwanami Shoten, 1925.

Nakada Kaoru. *Shōen no kenkyū* (Studies of the Shōen System). Tokyo: Shōkō Shoin, 1948.

Maki Kenji. *Nihon hōken seido seiritsushi* (History of the Formation of Japanese Feudalism). Kyoto: Kōbundō, 1935.
Study of feudalism in the Kamakura era.

Oae Ryō. *Hōkenteki shujusei seiritsushi kenkyū* (Studies of the Japanese Feudalistic Relationship of Master and Servant). Tokyo: Kazama Shobō, 1967.

Ishii Susumu. *Nihon chūsei kokkashi no kenkyū* (Study of the History of the Japanese Medieval State). Tokyo: Iwanami Shoten, 1970.

Satō Shin'ichi. *Kamakura bakufu shugo seido no kenkyū* (Studies of the Shugo System of the Kamakura Bakufu). Tokyo: Kaname Shobō, 1948. Rev. ed.: *Zōtei Kamakura bakufu shugo seido no kenkyū* Tokyo: University of Tokyo Press, 1971.

————. *Muromachi bakufu shugo seido no kenkyūjo* (Studies of the Shugo System of the Muromachi Bakufu vol. 1). Tokyo: University of Tokyo Press, 1967.

Aida Jirō. *Chūsei no sekisho* (Barrier Posts in the Middle Ages). Tokyo: Unebi Shobō, 1943.

Ishii Ryōsuke. *Chūsei buke fudōsan soshōhō no kenkyū* (A Study of Procedural Law of Real Actions in the Bakufu Courts of the Middle Ages). Tokyo: Kōbundō, 1938.

Satō Shin'ichi. *Kamakura bakufu soshō seido no kenkyū* (Studies of the Judicial System of the Kamakura Bakufu). Tokyo: Unebi Shobō, 1943.

Ishii Ryōsuke. *Nihon fudōsan sen'yū ron—chūsei ni okeru chigyō no ken-*

kyū (Japanese Possession of Real Property: A Study of the Chigyō of the Middle Ages). Tokyo: Sōbunsha, 1952.
The author describes *chigyō*, a form of possession peculiar to Japan, as an intermediate form between *possesio* in Roman law and *gewere* in German law.

VI. Kinsei

Kobayashi, Hiroshi. *Dateke jinkaishū no kenkyū* (A Study of the Jinkaishū of the Date Family). Tokyo: Sōbunsha, 1970.

Inoue, Kazuo. *Chōsokabe okitegaki no kenkyū* (A Study of Chōsokabe Okitegaki). Kōchi-shi Shimin Toshokan (Kōchi City Municipal Library), 1955.

Matsudaira Tarō. *Edo jidai seido no kenkyū, jō-kan* (A Study of the Edo Judiciary System) I. Bukeseido Kenkyūkai, 1919. Rev. ed.: *Edo jidai seido no kenkyū*. Tokyo: Kashiwa Shobō, 1964.

Maeda Masaharu. *Nihon kinsei sonpō no kenkyū furoku: sonpō-shū* (Study of Villages Laws in Early Modern Japan. Appendix: Village Laws). Tokyo: Yūhikaku, 1950.

Nakada Kaoru. *Mura oyobi iriai no kenkyū* (Study of Villages and Commons). Tokyo: Iwanami Shoten, 1949.

Andō Hiroshi. *Tokugawa bakufu kenji yōryaku* (Outline of the Administration of Tokugawa Shogunate-Controlled Territories). Tokyo: Seiabō, 1965.

Hiramatsu Yoshirō. *Kinsei keiji shoshōhō no kenkyū* (Study of the Law of Criminal Procedure in the Early Modern Period). Tokyo: Sōbunsha, 1960.

Kobayakawa Kingo. *Kinsei minji shoshō seido no kenkyū* (Study of the System of Civil Procedure in the Early Modern Period). Tokyo: Yūhikaku, 1957.

Ishii Ryōsuke. *Edo no keibatsu* (Punishments in the Edo Era). *Chūkō shinsho* (New Series of Chūō Kōronsha). Tokyo: Chūō Kōron, 1964.

Ninsoku Yoseba Kenshōkai, ed., *Ninsoku Yoseba shi* (A History of Ninsoku Yoseba). Tokyo: Sōbunsha, 1969.

Nakada Kaoru. *Tokugawa jidai no bungaku ni mietaru shihō* (Private

Law as Revealed in the Literature of the Tokugawa Period). Tokyo: Sōbunsha, 1956.

Miyamoto Mataji. *Kabunakama no kenkyū* (Study of the Kabunakama), 1938. Revised ed.: Tokyo: Yūhikaku, 1958.

Hozumi Shigetō. *Enkirijō to enkiridera* (Notes on Divorce and Divorce Temples). Tokyo: Nihon Hyōronsha, 1943.

Ishii Ryōsuke. *Edo jidai manpitsu* (A Miscellany on the Edo Era), 6 vols. Tokyo: Inoue Shobō, 1959–64.

VII. Kindai

Ishii Ryōsuke. *Meiji bunkashi—hōsei hen* (History of Meiji Culture: Legislation). *Meiji bunkashi* (History of Meiji Culture) 2. Tokyo: Yōyōsha, 1954.

Translated and adapted by William J. Chambliss: *Japanese Legislation in the Meiji Era* (Tokyo: Panpacific Press, 1958).

Kobayakawa Kingo. *Meiji hōseishi ron—kōhō no bu* (Legal History of the Meiji Era: Public Laws) 2 Vols. Tokyo: Ganshōdō Shoten, 1940.

Inada Masatsugu. *Meiji kenpō seiritsushi* (History of the Compilation of the Meiji Constitution) Vol. I, 1960; Vol. II, 1962. Tokyo: Yūhikaku.

Fukushima Masao. *Chiso kaisei no kenkyū* (A Study of Revision of the Land Tax). Tokyo: Yūhikaku, 1962.

Matsushita Yoshio. *Meiji gunseishi ron* (History of the Meiji Military System). 2 vols. Tokyo: Yūhikaku, 1956.

Tetsuka Yutaka. *Meiji shoki keihōshi no kenkyū* (Study of the History of Criminal Laws of Early Meiji). Tokyo: Keio Gijuku Daigaku Hōgaku Kenkyūkai (Keio University Law Association), 1956.

Kainō Michitaka. *Iriai no kenkyū* (Study of Commons). Tokyo: University of Tokyo Press, 1953.

Shinmi Kichiji. *Jinshinkoseki seiritsu ni kansuru kenkyū* (A Study of the Formation of *Jinshinkoseki*). Tokyo: Japan Society for the Promotion of Science, 1959.

Takayanagi Shinzō. *Meiji kazokuhōshi* (A History of the Meiji Law Governing Family Rights). *Hōritsugaku taikei* (Series on

Jurisprudence) Part 2: *Hōgaku riron hen* (Legal Theory) 83. Tokyo: Nihon Hyōronsha, 1951.

Ukai Nobushige, Fukushima Masao, Kawashima Takeyoshi, and Tsuji Kiyoaki, eds. *Kōza Nihon kindaihō hattatsushi* (Lecture Series: A History of the Development of Modern Japanese Law), 11 volumes (present). Tokyo: Keisō Shobō, 1958–67.

INDEX

Abe Nobuyuki (prime minister), 123
administration: under Hideyoshi, 72–
73; under Edo *bakufu*, 73. *See also*
local administration
Aikokusha (Patriotic Society), 107
Aki *han*, anti-*bakufu* activities of, 96
Amaterasu-ōmikami, 6, 8
Amended Criminal Code and Statutes (*Kaitei Ritsurei*) (1873), 92,
111, 117
Amenoshita-shiroshimesu-sumeramikoto
(title of the emperor), 9–11
ancient period, 17–30
anti-*bakufu* thought, 80–81
Antimonopoly Law (*Dokusen Kinshi
Hō*), 129
archaic period, 3–16; law and religion as indistinguishable during,
3; penal law during, 10–11; relations with other countries during,
13; control of land during, 13–14
Ashikaga Takauji (*shōgun*), 48, 49, 50

bakufu. *See* Edo *bakufu*; Kamakura
bakufu; Muromachi *bakufu*
Boissonade, G. E., 118
bourgeois culture, rise of, 70
buke (warrior houses), 34
buke ho (law pertaining to warrior
domains), 46
buke no tōryō (chief of the warrior
houses), 38, 48, 55, 95; emperor
as, 96
Buke sho-hatto (code of conduct for
warriors), 54, 66, 68, 71

bushi (warrior class), emergence of,
26, 31, 37–38

Cabinet (*naikaku*), 113; formation of
by the emperor, 115; formation of
by political parties, 115, 120; formation of outside the political
system, 122
capital: movement of, 13, 20; in
Settsu, 20; in Nara, 22; in Kyoto,
29; in Edo (Tokyo), 99; administration of, 26
castle-towns (*jōkamachi*), 57, 64, 67,
76
Charter Oath (1868), 98, 103, 105
China: relations with, 13, 19, 112;
war with (1894–95), 119; invasion
of, 120–21
China Incident (1937), 123, 125
Chinese influence: on culture, 9, 19,
22–23; on legal system, 23, 24, 91–
92; on Meiji-era law, 111–12, 117
Chōshū (Nagato *han*), 86, 95; anti-
bakufu activities of, 96, 97; importance of in Meiji government, 100–
101, 102, 106; role of in early party
governments, 116
chō tax, 12, 28, 36
Chūai (14th emperor), 8, 9
cities: during *sengoku* era, 57; during
Edo era, 76
Civil Code, 92, 118
class system: establishment of by
Hideyoshi, 64; reform of by Meiji
government, 110–11